Internet Research

ILLUSTRATED, Fourth Edition

Internet Research

ILLUSTRATED, Fourth Edition

Donald I. Barker
Carol D. Terry

COURSE TECHNOLOGY
CENGAGE Learning

Australia • Brazil • Japan • Korea • Mexico • Singapore • Spain • United Kingdom • United States

COURSE TECHNOLOGY
CENGAGE Learning

Internet Research—Illustrated, Fourth Edition
Donald I. Barker and Carol D. Terry

Executive Editor: Marjorie Hunt

Senior Product Manager: Christina Kling Garrett

Associate Product Manager: Rebecca Padrick

Editorial Assistant: Michelle Camisa

Marketing Director: Cheryl Costantini

Marketing Manager: Ryan DeGrote

Product Marketing Specialist: Jennifer Hankin

Developmental Editor: Barbara Clemens

Senior Content Project Manager: Jill Braiewa

Art Director: Kun-Tee Chang

Print Buyer: Fola Orekoya

Text Designer: Joseph Lee, Black Fish Design

Proofreader: Karen Annett

Indexer: Sharon Hilgenberg

QA Reviewers: Nicole Ashton, John Freitas,
    Jeff Schwartz, Susan Whalen

Cover Artist: Mark Hunt

Compositor: GEX Publishing Services

For product information and technology assistance, contact us at
Cengage Learning Customer & Sales Support, 1-800-354-9706
For permission to use material from this text or product, submit all requests online at
cengage.com/permissions
Further permissions questions can be emailed to
permissionrequest@cengage.com

ISBN-13: 978-1-4239-9942-3

ISBN-10: 1-4239-9942-8

Course Technology
25 Thomson Place
Boston, MA 02210
USA

Cengage Learning is a leading provider of customized learning solutions with office locations around the globe, including Singapore, the United Kingdom, Australia, Mexico, Brazil, and Japan. Locate your local office at: **international.cengage.com/region**

Cengage Learning products are represented in Canada by Nelson Education, Ltd.

For your lifelong learning solutions, visit **course.cengage.com**
Purchase any of our products at your local college store or at our preferred online store
www.ichapters.com

Figures A-7, A-8, A-11, A-13, A-14, A-15, A-15 Courtesy of Google. Google™ is a trademark of Google Inc. (www.google.com), Figures A-9, A-10 Courtesy of Microsoft Corporation. Microsoft product screen shots reprinted with permission from Microsoft Corporation, Figure A-19 Courtesy of HowStuff Works.com (www.howstuffworks.com), Figure A-25 Courtesy of Library and Archives Canada (www.collectioncandand .ca) , Figures B-3, B-5, B-7, B-11, B-13, B-14, B-21, B-22, B-24 Courtesy of Google. Google™ is a trademark of Google Inc. (www.google.com), Figures B-15, B-16 Courtesy of ixquick (www.ixquick .com), Figure B-24 Reproduced with permission of Yahoo! Inc. YAHOO! And the YAHOO! Logo are trademarks of Yahoo! Inc (www.yahoo.com), Figure B-26 Courtesy of Jon Vinton, BobbyMooreOnline (www.bobbymoore online .co.uk), Figures C-1, C-2, C-19 Courtesy of Librarians' Internet Index (LII) (www.ill.org), Figures C-3, C-5 Courtesy of Scout Archives, copyright 2008 Internet Scout Project (http://scout.wisc.edu), Figures C-4, C-6, C-22 © 1998-2008 Netscape Communications Corporation. Used with permission (www.dmoz.com), Figures C-7, C-8 Courtesy of BUBL Information Service (bubl.ac.uk), Figures C-9, C-10, C-11 Courtesy of the U.S. Department of Energy (DOC), Energy Efficiency and Renewable Energy (EERE) (www.eere.energy.gov), Figures C-12, C-13, C-14 Courtesy of the Source for Renewable Energy, Momentum Technologies LLC (energy.sourceguides.com), Figure C-16 Courtesy of the Database of State Incentives for Renewable Energy, DSIRE, a project of the North Carolina Solar Center at North Carolina State University and the Inter state Renewable Energy Council (IREC) (www.dsireusa.org), Figure C-17 Courtesy of Planet 21, an independent non-profit company and a registered British charity (peopleandplanet.net), Figure C-18 Courtesy of the University of California, Riverside (infomine.ucr.edu), Figure C-20 Courtesy of Northwestern Univer sity Library (www.library .northwestern.edu), Figure C-21 Courtesy of the National Health Information Center, U.S. Department of Health and Human Services (www.healthfinder.gov), Figure C-23 Courtesy of HowStat Computing Services (www.howstat.com.au), Figures D-2, D-3, D-4, D-15, D-17, D-18 Reproduced with permission of Yahoo! Inc. YAHOO! And the YAHOO! Logo are trademarks of Yahoo! Inc (www. yahoo.com) , Figures D-5, D-6, D-7 Courtesy of Idearc Media Corp., home of Superpages.com, Figures D-8, D-9, D-19 Courtesy of Hot Neuron LLC (www.magportal.com), Figures D-10, D-11 Courtesy of USA.gov, Office of Citizen Services and Communications, U.S. General Services Administration (www.USA.gov), Figures D-12, D-13 Courtesy of The Internet Public Library (www.ipl.org), Figures D-14, D-23 Courtesy of Blinkx (www.blinkx.com), Figures D-16, D-20 Courtesy of Google. Google™ is a trademark of Google Inc. (www. google.com), Figure D-21 Courtesy of Telstra Corporation Limited (yellowpages.com.au). Yellow Pages and Yellow are Australian registered trade marks of Telstra Corporation Limited., Figure D-22 Map Quest and the MapQuest logo are registered trademarks of MapQuest, Inc. Map content © 2008 by Map Quest, Inc and it's respective copyright holders. Used with permission., Figure D-24 Copyright © [2008] Globe Newspaper Company (boston.com)

Printed in China by China Translation & Printing Services Limited
2 3 4 5 6 7 14 13 12 11 10 09

About This Book

Welcome to *Internet Research—Illustrated, Fourth Edition*! Since the first book in the Illustrated Series was published in 1994, millions of students have used various Illustrated texts to master software skills and learn computer concepts. We are proud to bring you this brand new Illustrated book that is updated to included the latest information on how to perform research using Internet search tools.

This new edition shows how to take advantage of the most talked about, exciting, and powerful developments in search technology: *vertical search* and *social search*. Students will learn how to use the most powerful vertical search tools to easily and quickly locate specific types of media and content, such as video, audio, images, news, and so on. In addition, this new edition describes how *blended (universal) search* is emerging as a means to view one comprehensive result, containing a mix of such media as video, photos, PDF files, maps, and news content.

Students will also explore how to use social search to tap the power of collaborative human judgment and opinion to answer their questions and provide informed guidance. They will discover the benefits and limitations of blogs, social bookmarking, collaborative harvesters, and question & answer sites. In addition, students will learn about Wikis, server software that lets anyone easily build and interlink Web pages, encouraging group participation in building Web content.

This book's unique design, which presents each skill on two facing pages, makes it easy for novices to absorb and understand new skills, and also makes it easy for more experienced computer users to progress through the lessons quickly, with minimal reading required. We are confident that this book and all its available resources will help your students master the latest techniques in finding information and performing research on the Internet.

Author Acknowledgments

Donald I. Barker and Carol D. Terry Creating a book is a team effort. We would like to thank: our spouses, Chia-Ling Barker and Paul Turner, for their unfailing patience and generous support; Marjorie Hunt for publishing the book; Christina Kling Garrett for managing the project; and our excellent developmental editor, Barbara Clemens, for corrections and invaluable suggestions.

Preface

Welcome to *Internet Research—Illustrated, Fourth Edition.* If this is your first experience with the Illustrated series, you'll see that this book has a unique design: each skill is presented on two facing pages, with steps on the left and screens on the right. The layout makes it easy to digest a skill without having to read a lot of text and flip pages to see an illustration.

This book is an ideal learning tool for a wide range of learners—the rookies will find the clean design easy to follow and focused with only essential information presented, and the hotshots will appreciate being able to move quickly through the lessons to find the information they need without reading a lot of text. The design also makes this a great reference after the course is over! See the illustration on the right to learn more about the pedagogical and design elements of a typical lesson.

What's New in This Edition

We've made many changes and enhancements to this edition to make it the best ever. Here are some highlights of what's new:

- **Redesigned Unit Opener Page**—The first page of each unit now includes a listing of all the Data Files that are needed for the unit.

- **Real Life Independent Challenge**—The new Real Life Independent Challenge exercises offer students the opportunity to use the Internet to research ways to help find a job, including: researching employability skills; using vertical search engines to find advice on job interview skills; how to chart a career; and help preparing a resume.

Each two-page spread focuses on a single skill.

Concise text introduces the basic principles in the lesson.

UNIT A
Internet Research

Citing Online Resources

When you use information from Web pages for classwork, you need to list them in your works cited. Even if your research is not for school, it is a good idea to gather enough information about each Web page so that you, or someone reading your work, can find it later. To present the relevant data about each site consistently, use a recognized citation format. **Citation formats** are style guides that standardize how citations are written. Two widely accepted citation formats are those of the Modern Language Association (MLA) and the American Psychological Association (APA). These style guides provide formats for all kinds of Internet information. For academic work, always check with your instructor to see which style guide format is preferred. See Table A-3 for citation tips. Bob advises you to use the MLA format to record citations for the Web pages you are finding in a way that will make your list consistent and easy for you or your colleagues to find again.

STEPS

> **QUICK TIP**
> To learn more, go to the Online Companion at www.course.com/illustrated/research4 for citation guide links, under "Other resources."

1. **Review Figure A-17, which shows the elements of an MLA citation format**
   Figure A-18 shows an example MLA citation, and Figure A-19 shows part of the Web page cited in the example.

2. **Locate the author named in Figure A-19, then type the name in the Citing Online Resources table in your document**
   MLA format for author names is surname (last name) first, followed by a comma, then the personal name (first name) followed by a period. Note that many Web pages do not display this information as clearly as the example. You might have to look to find it and it might not be provided at all.

3. **Locate the title of the Web page in Figure A-19 and type it in the same table**
   MLA format requires quotation marks around the title with a period at the end of the title.

4. **Find the title of the Web site and type it in the same table**
   MLA format requires the title be underlined and followed by a period.

5. **Look for the date the Web page was created or the date it was last updated**
   As in this example, sometimes there is no creation/update date and you must skip this step.

> **QUICK TIP**
> The URL for any Web page is visible in the browser's address bar, but is not shown in Figure A-19.

6. **Type http://science.howstuffworks.com/solar-cell.htm in the same table in your document**
   The URL (Internet address) should be enclosed in angle brackets < > and should not be underlined.

7. **Type the date that you view this Web page in the same table**
   MLA format for dates is *DD Month Abbreviation YYYY* followed by a period. For example: 15 Oct. 2008. It is important to record the date you view a Web page because pages are changed frequently.

> **QUICK TIP**
> Be sure to use all of the required punctuation.

8. **Compare your citation with the example in Figure A-18, make corrections as needed, then save, print, and close the document**

Copyright and plagiarism

With the exception of works in the public domain, everything on the Internet is copyrighted, whether it is a Web page, an image, or an audio file. If you want to profit from someone else's work, you must get permission from the author or creator. Copyright law is very complex, so consult a lawyer who specializes in copyright law. If you want to use part of someone else's work in a school assignment or paper, you generally can do so under the Fair Use exemption to copyright law. "Fair use" allows students and researchers to copy or use parts of other people's work for educational purposes. Always give credit by citing the source of the material you are using. If you don't credit an author or source, you are guilty of plagiarism. For more information, see "Other resources" in the Online Companion.

Internet Research 16   Searching the Internet Effectively

Hints as well as troubleshooting tips appear right where you need them—next to the step itself.

Clues to Use boxes provide concise information that expands on the lesson skill or describes a related task.

vi

Every lesson features large, full-color representations of what the screen should look like as students complete the numbered steps.

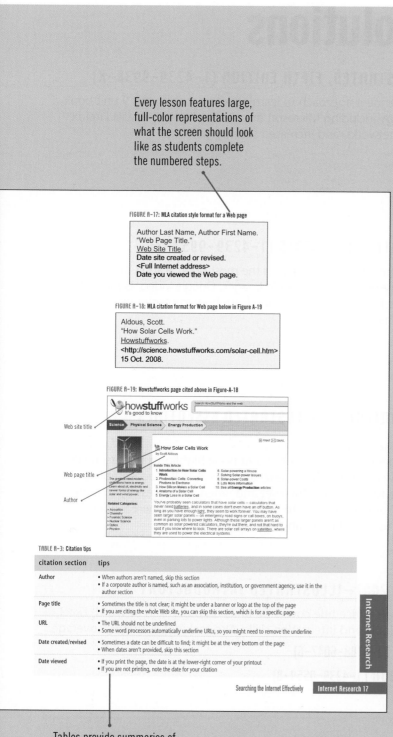

FIGURE A-17: MLA citation style format for a Web page

Author Last Name, Author First Name.
"Web Page Title."
Web Site Title.
Date site created or revised.
<Full Internet address>
Date you viewed the Web page.

FIGURE A-18: MLA citation format for Web page below in Figure A-19

Aldous, Scott.
"How Solar Cells Work."
Howstuffworks.
<http://science.howstuffworks.com/solar-cell.htm>
15 Oct. 2008.

FIGURE A-19: Howstuffworks page cited above in Figure A-18

TABLE A-3: Citation tips

citation section	tips
Author	• When authors aren't named, skip this section • If a corporate author is named, such as an association, institution, or government agency, use it in the author section
Page title	• Sometimes the title is not clear; it might be under a banner or logo at the top of the page • If you are citing the whole Web site, you can skip this section, which is for a specific page
URL	• The URL should not be underlined • Some word processors automatically underline URLs, so you might need to remove the underline
Date created/revised	• Sometimes a date can be difficult to find; it might be at the very bottom of the page • When dates aren't provided, skip this section
Date viewed	• If you print the page, the date is at the lower-right corner of your printout • If you are not printing, note the date for your citation

Searching the Internet Effectively   Internet Research 17

Tables provide summaries of key terms, buttons, or keyboard shortcuts connected with the lesson material.

Assignments

The assignments on the light purple pages at the end of each unit increase in difficulty. Additional case studies provide a variety of interesting and relevant exercises for students to practice skills. Assignments include:

• **Concepts Reviews** consist of multiple choice, matching, and screen identification questions.

• **Skills Reviews** provide additional hands-on, step-by-step reinforcement.

• **Independent Challenges** are case projects requiring critical thinking and application of the unit skills. The Independent Challenges increase in difficulty, with the first one in each unit being the easiest. Independent Challenges 2 and 3 become increasingly open-ended, requiring more independent problem solving.

• **Real Life Independent Challenges** are practical exercises to help students with their every day lives.

• **Advanced Challenge Exercises** set within the Independent Challenges provide optional steps for more advanced students.

• **Visual Workshops** are practical, self-graded capstone projects that require independent problem solving.

Other Training Solutions

THE INTERNET—ILLUSTRATED, FIFTH EDITION (1-4239-9938-X)

Offering a browser-independent approach to learning internet skills, this 9 unit book covers the latest technology including Microsoft Internet Explorer 7, Mozilla Firefox, messaging, online social networks, and increased security coverage.

GOOGLE™—ILLUSTRATED ESSENTIALS (1-4239-9953-3)

Our 2 unit book has students get interactive with the most popular tools from Google including advanced Google search tools, Google Images, Google Video, Google News, Google Maps, and Google Earth. Students will also learn how to communicate with Gmail and update and enhance their blog.

COPYRIGHT ON THE INTERNET—ILLUSTRATED ESSENTIALS (1-4239-0551-2)

Framed as questions students might ask, this 2 unit book highlights the essentials of what they should know about copyright law, such as when it is acceptable to download and use media found on the Internet and when it is necessary to gain permission. Our Online Companion links to public domain sites where students can find media they can use or adapt in any way they wish.

MICROSOFT® OFFICE 2007—ILLUSTRATED INTRODUCTORY

Our Introductory Microsoft Office title covers 26 units on basic skills in Word, Excel, Access, PowerPoint, Outlook, and integration skills. Also includes Windows coverage.

WINDOWS XP EDITION (1-4188-6047-6)

WINDOWS VISTA EDITION (1-4239-0559-8)

MICROSOFT® OFFICE 2007—ILLUSTRATED INTRODUCTORY VIDEO (1-4239-9954-1)

Our new Video Companion is the "video version" of our bestselling Microsoft Office 2007 Introductory text, featuring 147 videos based on the Office lessons in the book. Designed to supplement the book, not replace it, the Video Companion contains 10 hours of video and provides a rich learning experience for all students.

For more titles from the Illustrated Series, visit www.course.com/illustrated.

Instructor Resources

The Instructor Resources CD is Course Technology's way of putting the resources and information needed to teach and learn effectively into your hands. With an integrated array of teaching and learning tools that offer you and your students a broad range of technology-based instructional options, we believe this CD represents the highest quality and most cutting edge resources available to instructors today. Many of these resources are available at *www.course.com*. The resources available with this book are:

- **Instructor's Manual**—Available as an electronic file, the Instructor's Manual includes detailed lecture topics with teaching tips for each unit.

- **Sample Syllabus**—Prepare and customize your course easily using this sample course outline.

- **PowerPoint Presentations**—Each unit has a corresponding PowerPoint presentation that you can use in lecture, distribute to your students, or customize to suit your course.

- **Figure Files**—The figures in the text are provided on the Instructor Resources CD to help you illustrate key topics or concepts. You can create traditional overhead transparencies by printing the figure files. Or you can create electronic slide shows by using the figures in a presentation program such as PowerPoint.

- **Solutions to Exercises**—Solutions to Exercises contains every file students are asked to create or modify in the lessons and end-of-unit material. Also provided in this section is a document outlining the solutions for the end-of-unit Concepts Review, Skills Review, and Independent Challenges.

- **Data Files for Students**—To complete most of the units in this book, your students will need Data Files. You can post the Data Files on a file server for students to copy. The Data Files are available on the Instructor Resources CD, the Review Pack, and can also be downloaded from *www.course.com*. In this edition, we have included a lesson on downloading the Data Files for this book on page xiv.

Instruct students to use the Data Files List included on the Review Pack and the Instructor Resources CD. This list gives instructions on copying and organizing files.

- **ExamView**—ExamView is a powerful testing software package that allows you to create and administer printed, computer (LAN-based), and Internet exams. ExamView includes hundreds of questions that correspond to the topics covered in this text, enabling students to generate detailed study guides that include page references for further review. The computer-based and Internet testing components allow students to take exams at their computers, and also saves you time by grading each exam automatically.

CourseCasts—Learning on the Go. Always Available... Always Relevant.

Want to keep up with the latest technology trends relevant to you? Visit our site to find a library of podcasts, CourseCasts, featuring a "CourseCast of the Week," and download them to your mp3 player at *http://coursecasts.course.com*.

Our fast-paced world is driven by technology. You know because you're an active participant—always on the go, always keeping up with technological trends, and always learning new ways to embrace technology to power your life.

Ken Baldauf, a faculty member of the Florida State University Computer Science Department, is responsible for teaching technology classes to thousands of FSU students each year. He knows what you know; he knows what you want to learn. He's also an expert in the latest technology and will sort through and aggregate the most pertinent news and information so you can spend your time enjoying technology, rather than trying to figure it out.

Visit us at *http://coursecasts.course.com* to learn on the go!

Brief Contents

Contents

Read This Before You Begin

Frequently Asked Questions

Are there any prerequisites for this book?

This book focuses on using the Internet effectively as a powerful research tool. It assumes that you are familiar with the Internet and Internet terms, and know basic Web-browsing skills. Basic Web-browsing skills include using the menus and toolbars in the browser of your choice, entering URLs, and navigating the Web using hyperlinks. In order to complete the exercises using the Data Files, you should also have basic word-processing skills.

What are Data Files?

A Data File is a file that you use to complete the steps in the units and exercises to create the final materials that you submit to your instructor. Each unit opener page lists the Data Files that you need for that unit.

Where are the Data Files?

Your instructor will provide the Data Files to you or direct you to a location on a network drive from which you can download them. Alternatively, you can follow the instructions on the next page to download the Data Files from this book's Web page.

Do I need to be connected to the Internet to complete the steps and exercises in this book?

Yes, you will need an Internet connection, a Web browser, and a text-editing or word-processing program such as Microsoft Word or WordPad, in order to complete the lessons and exercises in this book.

What is the Online Companion and how do I use it?

You use the Online Companion, located at www.course.com/illustrated/research4, to access all the links used in the book. Because the Internet and its search engines change frequently, the Online Companion will provide updates to the text as necessary. To access the Online Companion quickly, add the URL to your Favorites or Bookmarks, or set it as your home page. (If you are working in a lab, ask your instructor before doing this.) The URL is provided throughout the book in steps and tips for easy reference as well.

Downloading Data Files for This Book

In order to complete many of the lesson steps and exercises in this book, you are asked to open and save Data Files. A **Data File** is a partially completed file that you use as a starting point to complete the steps in the units and exercises. The benefit of using a Data File is that it saves you the time and effort needed to create a file; you can simply open a Data File, save it with a new name (so the original file remains intact), then make changes to it to complete lesson steps or an exercise. Your instructor will provide the Data Files to you or direct you to a location on a network drive from which you can download them. Alternatively, you can follow the instructions in this lesson to download the Data Files from this book's Web page.

1. Start Internet Explorer, type www.course.com in the address bar, then press [Enter]

2. When the Course.com Web site opens, click the Student Downloads link

3. On the Student Downloads page, click in the Search text box, type this book's ISBN: 9781423999423, then click Go

QUICK TIP
You can also click Student Downloads on the right side of the product page.

4. When the page opens for this textbook, in the left navigation bar, click the Download Student Files link, then, on the Student Downloads page, click the Data Files link

5. If the File Download – Security Warning dialog box opens, click Save. (If no dialog box appears, skip this step and go to Step 6)

TROUBLE
If a dialog box opens telling you that the download is complete, click Close.

6. If the Save As dialog box opens, click the Save in list arrow at the top of the dialog box, select a folder on your USB drive or hard disk to download the file to, then click Save

7. Close Internet Explorer and then open My Computer (Windows XP) or Computer (Windows Vista) or Windows Explorer and display the contents of the drive and folder to which you downloaded the file

8. Double-click the file 9942-3d.exe in the drive or folder, then, if the Open File – Security Warning dialog box opens, click Run

QUICK TIP
By default, the files will extract to C:\ CourseTechnology\ 9942-3d

9. In the WinZip Self-Extractor window, navigate to the drive and folder where you want to unzip the files to, then click Unzip

10. When the WinZip Self-Extractor displays a dialog box listing the number of files that have unzipped successfully, click OK, click Close in the WinZip Self-Extractor dialog box, then close Windows Explorer, My Computer, or Computer

You are now ready to open the required files.

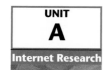

Searching the Internet Effectively

Finding lots of irrelevant and potentially unreliable information on the Internet is easier than finding information you want and trust. In this unit, you learn about search tools, strategies, analysis, and citations that maximize your chances of locating relevant content that meets your needs and citing it in a standard format. ▨▨▨ You work in the City Planning Office in Portland, Oregon. The city is working toward becoming more energy independent and you are to create a list of Web resources on alternative energy. Although you use the Web, you realize your skills need some polishing to do a quality job. You ask your friend, Bob Johnson, a reference librarian at a Portland university reference library, to help you learn the basics of Internet searching.

OBJECTIVES

Understand Internet search tools

Create an Internet research strategy

Identify the right keywords

Perform a basic search

Add keywords

Phrase search

Analyze search results

Cite online resources

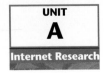
Understanding Internet Search Tools

The **World Wide Web** is an enormous repository of information stored on millions of computers all over the world. The **Internet** is a vast global network of interconnected smaller networks. You use the Internet to connect to information on the Web. You use **Internet search tools**, services that locate information on the Web, to find the information you need. Your **search query** tells the search tool specifically what information you want. Search tools can be divided into four major categories: search engines, metasearch engines, subject guides, and specialized search tools. Different search tools are better for finding different types of information, and no tool searches the entire Internet. Figure A-1 illustrates the four types of search tools and the areas of the Web they cover. ▰▰▰ Before you start your search for Web pages about alternative energy, Bob gives you a brief overview of search tools.

DETAILS

Types of search tools include the following:

QUICK TIP

To find out more about search engines, click the Search Engine Watch link or the Search Engine Showdown link on the Online Companion, under "Online references," at www.course.com/illustrated/research4.

- **Search engines** enable you to locate Web pages that contain keywords you enter in a search form. **Keywords** are the nouns and verbs, and sometimes important adjectives, that describe the major concepts of your search topic. A program called a **spider** crawls or scans the Web to index the keywords in Web pages. The indexes, or indices, created by spiders match the keywords you enter in a search engine and return a list of links to Web pages that contain these keywords. Because this is a precise process, it provides a narrow search of the Web and works well for finding specific content. Because spiders take months to index even a small portion of the Web, search engine results are limited and some might be out of date. No single search engine covers the entire Web, so consider using more than one engine for important searches.

- **Metasearch engines** offer a single search form to query multiple search engines simultaneously. As with search engines, you enter keywords to retrieve links to Web pages that contain matching information. Search results are compiled from other search engines, rather than from the Web. Metasearches are useful for quickly providing the highest ranked results from multiple search engines. Better metasearch engines remove duplicate results and rank the results based on relevancy to your query. Unfortunately, these results might not be optimal; the best search engines are often excluded from a metasearch because they charge fees, which metasearch engine providers decline to pay.

QUICK TIP

If you don't know much about the subject you need to research, a subject guide is often a good place to start online.

- **Subject guides** offer hierarchically organized topical directories that you navigate through to find relevant links. This design makes subject guides a good choice for a broad view of a topic. Subject guides are typically prepared by hand and vary in selectivity, criteria for inclusion, qualifications of human indexers, and levels of maintenance. Some are professional or academic sponsored, whereas others are commercial. Better subject guides also provide keyword searches of their database.

QUICK TIP

Major search engines constantly work toward being able to search parts of the Web that are currently invisible to their spiders.

- **Specialty search tools** allow you to find information that is "invisible" to traditional search engines or subject guides because it is stored in proprietary databases, specialty directories, or reference sites. The vast majority of the information on the Web is in this invisible area, usually called the **deep Web**. To retrieve this information, you must go to a specific site and use its unique search interface. Although many of these sites can be searched with specialty search tools, others require subscriptions or fees for access. Many of these are available at libraries.

FIGURE A-1: Internet search tools

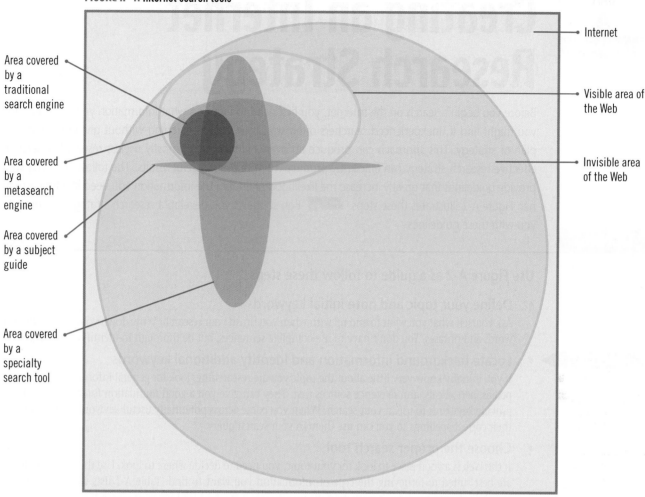

Internet

Area covered
by a
traditional
search engine

Visible area of
the Web

Area covered
by a
metasearch
engine

Invisible area
of the Web

Area covered
by a subject
guide

Area covered
by a
specialty
search tool

If this graphic were to scale, the area representing the invisible Web and the Internet would be dozens of times larger.

Using a search toolbar

Google, Live Search, and Yahoo! provide search toolbars that enable you to search the Internet from your desktop, or browser, without actually visiting the search engines. Although each toolbar is closely tied to its parent search engine, they share many features in common, such as the ability to block pop-ups, automatically complete forms, and protect against spyware. The Google Search Toolbar (http://toolbar. google.com/) checks the spelling of your queries, translates English words into other languages, and turns street addresses into links to online maps. The Live Search Toolbar (http://get.live.com/toolbar/overview) uses tabbed browsing to easily switch between Web pages and gives you one-click access to Hotmail, Windows Live Messenger, or Windows Live Spaces. The Yahoo! Search Toolbar (http://companion.yahoo.com/) provides one-click access to features on its site, such as My Yahoo!, mail, and news. The ixquick toolbar (http://us.ixquick.com/eng/aboutixquick/) provides quick metasearching and telephone directory searching, magnification buttons, and email emoticons.

Creating an Internet Research Strategy

Before you begin a search on the Internet, you first need to focus on what information you want and how you might find it. Inexperienced searchers often start their online searching without giving thought to a plan or strategy. This approach can produce an overwhelming list of mostly useless results. However, an effective research strategy can efficiently produce more relevant, useful results. The following seven steps provide guidelines that greatly increase the likelihood of finding the information you need in a timely manner. Figure A-2 illustrates these steps. 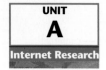 Bob suggests you develop a research strategy and provides you with these guidelines.

DETAILS

Use Figure A-2 as a guide to follow these steps:

- **Define your topic and note initial keywords**

  Ask yourself what you want to end up with when you finish your research. Write down your topic. Note keywords and phrases. You don't have to use complete sentences, but be thorough in identifying concepts.

QUICK TIP

If you get stuck at any point in your research, consult your local reference librarians. They are information experts.

- **Locate background information and identify additional keywords**

  If you initially know very little about the topic you are researching, look for general information in encyclopedias, periodicals, and reference sources first. They can give you a good foundation for your research and provide keywords to use in your search. When you come across potentially useful keywords, note them and their correct spellings so you can use them in your search query.

- **Choose the proper search tool**

  If the Web is a good place to look for your topic, you need to decide where to look. Use the search tools that are best suited to retrieving the type of information you want to find. Table A-1 lists the most common search tools and provides information on how to select the best tool for your research needs. If you want specific content, search engines or metasearch engines are appropriate. For a broader view, or when you know less about your topic, use subject guides. When seeking information not normally tracked by these tools, turn to specialty search tools. Combining these search tools provides the most thorough approach.

- **Translate your question into an effective search query**

  The first step in translating a question into an effective search query—which consists of a word, words, phrases, and symbols that a search engine can interpret—is to identify the keywords that best describe the topic. You use keywords to query either search engines or metasearch engines. You also use keywords to construct complex searches for even more accuracy.

- **Perform your search**

  Search engines offer a variety of different **search forms**, which contain fields in which you enter information specific to your search. Although some subject guides allow keyword searches, they are often searched by clicking through a series of links. In either case, the information you provide is used to return **search results**.

- **Evaluate your search results**

  The quantity and quality of results vary from one search engine to another. To ascertain the value of the information you find, you need to apply **evaluative criteria**, such as who authored the Web page or how current the information is.

- **Refine your search, if needed**

  You might need to go back to a previous step in the research process to refine your strategy if the quality or quantity of results is not what you need. Use what you learned from your first pass through this process to refine your search. First, try fine-tuning your search query, and then try a different search tool. If you are still not satisfied with your results, you might need to reevaluate your keywords. Perhaps they are too specific or obscure. If you are unable to do this or it isn't successful, you might need to seek more basic information on your topic. Or, rethink the topic—you might find that redefining it, based on what you have seen in your searches, would be helpful.

FIGURE A-2: Developing a research strategy

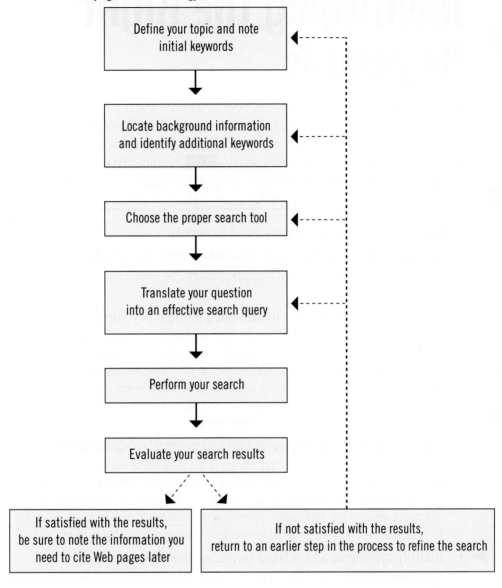

TABLE A-1: Common search tools (see the Online Companion for links)

search tool	best for	where it searches	how to search	sample information	sample tools
Search engines	General or specific	Searches its own indexes that are compiled from data gathered from the Web	Enter keywords, phrases, or complex searches	Alternative energy or solar panels	Google Yahoo! Live Search
Metasearch engines	General or specific	Searches the indexes of multiple search engines simultaneously	Enter keywords, phrases, or complex searches	Alternative energy or solar panels	ixquick Vivisimo metacrawler
Subject guides	More general	Searches its own files or database	Click through subject categories (might also allow keyword searches)	Alternative energy	Librarians' Internet Index ipl Scout Archives
Specialized tools	More specific	Searches databases, directories, reference sites, government information, media, and search engines	Enter keywords, phrases, or complex searches	Latest news on solar panels	USA.gov SuperPages MagPortal

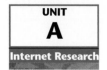

Identifying the Right Keywords

After identifying your research topic, you need to translate it into a search strategy that optimizes your chances of finding useful information. The main elements in your search strategy are the keywords that describe the major concepts of your search topic. It is these keywords that you enter into the search tool and which the search tool uses to return results. Bob provides you with the following guidelines to help you create a list of keywords to use in your search for Web resources on alternative energy.

DETAILS

Follow these guidelines to create a list of keywords:

- **Write a sentence or two that summarizes your research topic**

  You want to find Web resources on alternative energy. The sentence shown in Figure A-3 demonstrates how to state your research topic.

- **Study the research topic and pull out potential keywords**

  You look at this topic and decide the words that could be used as keywords are *alternative* and *energy*. You circle these words, as shown in Figure A-4. By identifying these words, you are starting to turn your topic statement into terms that an Internet search tool can use effectively. Remember, these are the words you expect to appear on the Web pages that might be useful for your project. Search engines normally do not search for the words *a*, *an*, and *the*, so you should not include them in most searches. See Table A-2 for typical words that do not qualify as keywords, also known as **stop words**.

- **If necessary, define the keywords and find general background information on your topic**

  If you know very little about the topic you are researching, some initial research can help you identify useful keywords. You look in a dictionary and see that alternative energy is considered energy from nonfossil fuels. It mentions *solar* and *wind* as examples. You then look in an encyclopedia to read a bit more about alternative energy. You find other types of alternative energies that might be useful, including *water*, *biomass*, and *geothermal*. Figure A-5 illustrates how to list the keywords you identified for your research topic.

- **Identify synonyms and related terms for the keywords**

  Synonyms are words that have similar meanings. The meanings don't have to be exactly the same, just close. Useful Web pages have likely been created by many different people, using different words to describe the same topic. By expanding your list of keywords, you help ensure that your queries are broad enough to find Web pages not indexed under the exact keywords in your initial list. Figure A-6 demonstrates how to list your identified synonyms and related terms.

QUICK TIP

As you review search results, keep this list of keywords and synonyms handy. You might find new words that might be useful if you refine your search later. You can use the list to keep track of which words you've searched as you try different search tools. Also, the words can help you identify topics in the pages you find.

TABLE A-2: Common words that are not useful in most searches

parts of speech	examples
Articles	a, an, the
Conjunctions and prepositions	and, or, but, in, of, for, on, into, from, than, at, to
Adjectives and adverbs	as, also, probably, however, very
Pronouns and verbs	this, that, these, those, is, be, see, do

FIGURE A-3: Write down your research topic statement

I want to find Web resources on alternative energy

FIGURE A-4: Circle the keywords in your statement

I want to find Web resources on (alternative) (energy)

FIGURE A-5: Identify and list additional keywords

Keywords

alternative

energy

solar

wind

water

biomass

geothermal

FIGURE A-6: Identify synonyms and related words

Keywords	Synonyms & Related Terms
alternative	renewable, sustainable
energy	power
solar	panels, photovoltaic
wind	turbines, windmills
water	hydropower, hydroelectric
biomass	waste-to-energy, bioenergy
geothermal	heat, pumps

Performing a Basic Search

Search engines often differ in how they perform a basic search. It is always a good idea to view each search engine's Help page before you use it. An effective search statement at one search engine might not produce the best results at another. You can overcome these inconsistencies by using a trial-and-error approach to searching. At each search engine, try subtle variations on the search, changing your wording slightly. Note which search engines perform best for different kinds of searches. ▰▰▰▰ You are ready to conduct a basic search using keywords you identified for alternative energy.

1. **Start your word-processing program, open the file IR A-1.doc from the drive and folder where you store your Data Files, then add your name at the top of the document**

   You can use this document to keep track of your search results. It is organized by lesson. You use the same document throughout the lessons in a unit, switching between the document and your browser as necessary.

2. **Click File on the menu bar, click Save As, navigate to the location where you are saving files for this book, then save the document as Searching the Internet**

3. **Start your Web browser, go to the Online Companion at www.course.com/illustrated/ research4, then click the Google link (under "Search engines")**

   The Google search form opens, as shown in Figure A-7.

4. **Click in the Search text box, type solar energy, then click Google Search**

   Your results should look similar to Figure A-8. Be aware that many search engines accept payment for higher placement, so these sites are listed where you typically expect the best matching results. Better search engines indicate this, sometimes with the word "Sponsored." However, they are not required to disclose this.

5. **In the Performing a Basic Search table in your document, record how many results were found, delete your previous query in the Search text box, type solar power, then click Search**

   Notice that the browser displays a different number of results for this search than the last. One small change in a search query can radically change the number and quality of search results. Also, note that the number of results displayed often includes multiple pages per site; that is, a site with multiple pages on your topic might be returned more than once in your results.

6. **Record the number of results in the same table in your document**

   You know that using a different search tool can alter results, so you decide to try your search using AltaVista.

7. **Go to the Online Companion, then click the AltaVista Search link (under "Search engines")**

8. **Click in the Search text box, type solar energy, click Find, then record the number of results this search found in the same table**

9. **Delete your previous query in the Search text box, type solar power, press [Enter], record the number of pages this search found in the same table, then save your document**

   Notice again that your browser displays a different number of results for this search than the last.

FIGURE A-7: Google search form

Links to other kinds of searches (Web search is the default selection)

Search text box

Search button

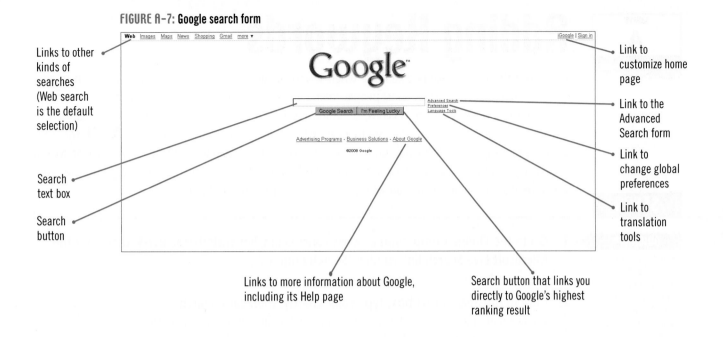

Link to customize home page

Link to the Advanced Search form

Link to change global preferences

Link to translation tools

Links to more information about Google, including its Help page

Search button that links you directly to Google's highest ranking result

FIGURE A-8: Google search results

Your search

Search results

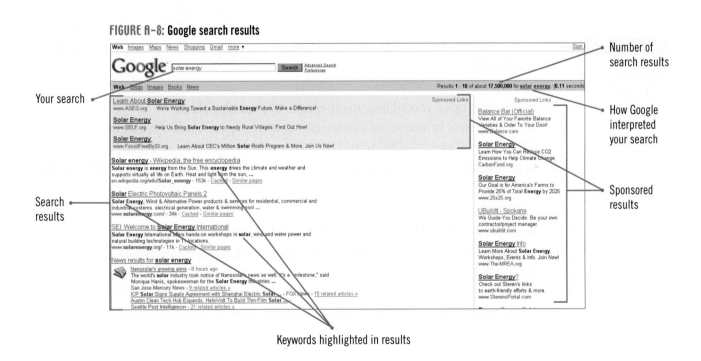

Number of search results

How Google interpreted your search

Sponsored results

Keywords highlighted in results

Why do search results vary with different search engines?

When a search engine spider scans the Internet for Web pages, it finds only a fraction of the Web pages that exist for any given topic. Each engine's spiders crawl different parts of the Web and a different scope of content. So when you use a different search engine, you are actually searching a slightly different part and a slightly different range of the Web. Also, each search engine has unique ranking algorithms. So when your results are ranked for relevancy, different search engines might list similar results in a different order.

Adding Keywords

The most common mistake people make when searching the Internet is using too few keywords to adequately describe a topic. In fact, most people enter a single keyword when performing a search, which typically returns thousands, if not millions, of search results. Entering several keywords, which narrows or focuses your search results, enables you to locate relevant information more efficiently. ⬛⬛⬛ You want to locate more specific information on developing a solar energy plan for Portland, so you decide to add some keywords to your search. You also want to find out whether adding keywords really improves your search results, so you decide to start with a basic search term, then add to it.

STEPS

QUICK TIP
Your browser should be open and the Searching the Internet document should be open in your word processor.

1. **Go to the Online Companion at www.course.com/illustrated/research4, then click the Microsoft Live Search link (under "Search engines")**

   The search form for Live Search opens.

2. **Click in the Search text box, type solar energy, then click Search**

   Figure A-9 illustrates your results. A count of the total results appears just below the Search text box, and is followed by a list of sponsored links and then the first page of results.

3. **In the Adding Keywords table in your document, record how many results this search found**

   The number of results is quite large and the page descriptions are not particularly relevant to using solar energy as an alternative power source for a city. You decide to add the keyword "city" to your query.

QUICK TIP
Web sites are redesigned frequently. Your screen may look a bit different.

4. **In the Search text box, click after the keyword energy, press [Spacebar], type city, then click Search**

   Figure A-10 illustrates your results.

5. **In the same table, record how many results this search yielded**

   This search returns far fewer results. In addition, the page descriptions indicate that the information is more closely related to solar energy use in a city.

6. **In the Search text box, click after the keyword city, press [Spacebar], type develop, then click Search**

   The number of results is now even smaller and more closely related to how to develop solar energy for a city.

7. **In the same table, record the number of results found by this search**

8. **In the Search text box, click after the keyword develop, press [Spacebar], type plan, then click Search**

   Your number of results is now even more limited and likely to be more relevant for your project.

9. **In the same table, record the number of results, then save your document**

FIGURE A-9: Live Search results

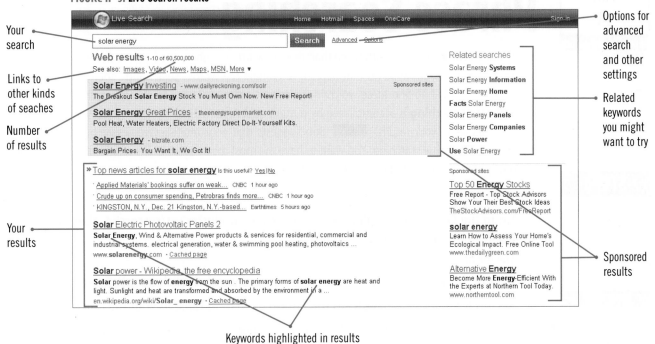

Your search

Links to other kinds of seaches

Number of results

Your results

Options for advanced search and other settings

Related keywords you might want to try

Sponsored results

Keywords highlighted in results

FIGURE A-10: Live Search results narrowed

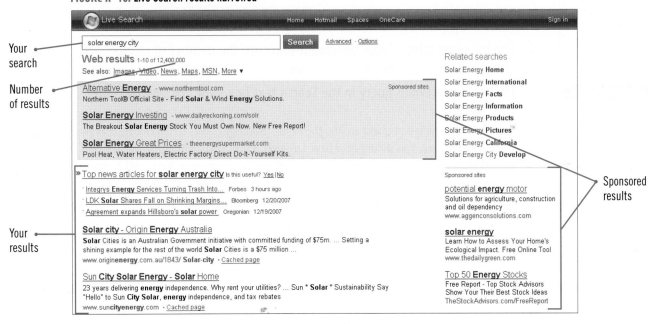

Your search

Number of results

Your results

Sponsored results

Arranging keywords

The order in which you place keywords in a search can be very important. Placing your most important keywords at the beginning of your search query causes a search engine to display documents featuring the more important keywords at the top of your search results. For example, the keywords *hybrid electric vehicle* cause a search engine to first look for documents containing the word "hybrid," then "electric," and, finally, "vehicle." Reversing the order of this search query (that is, *vehicle electric hybrid*) puts less emphasis on the keywords "hybrid" and "electric," hence changing the sequence of your search results. Depending on the search engine's algorithms, it might also change the number of your search results.

Phrase Searching

When you construct a search with more than one keyword, you often need two or more words to be in a phrase. For example, some pages that happen to contain the words "solar" and "energy" aren't actually about "solar energy." To find these words in the correct order, you need to phrase search. In many search tools, **phrase searching** is accomplished by putting quotation marks (" ") around the words you want to appear together in your results. Bob suggests that your multi-keyword searches can be refined even more with phrase searching. You want to have the most meaningful results returned, so you decide to try some phrase searches and compare the results.

STEPS

1. **Go to the Online Companion at www.course.com/illustrated/research4, then click the Google link (under "Search engines")**

   The search form for Google opens.

2. **Click in the Search text box, type bioenergy center, then click Google Search**

3. **Record the number of results in the Phrase Searching table in your document**

4. **Delete the previous query in the Search text box, type center bioenergy, then click Search**

   Figure A-11 illustrates your results for the two-keyword search. You should have approximately the same number of results as in your previous search. If *center bioenergy* and *bioenergy center* find close to the same number of results, you know that you have not limited your search to just the phrase *bioenergy center*. In a tool indexing millions of pages, this test's results can vary by a larger number than when using a tool such as a subject guide, which would be more likely to return identical results.

5. **Use the same table in your document to record the number of results**

   You now use phrase searching to limit your results.

6. **Delete your previous query in the Search text box, type "bioenergy center", then click Search**

   Be sure to type quotation marks around the words *"bioenergy center"* to tell Google that you mean to search for an exact phrase. You should now have far fewer results than in the first two searches. This search has located only Web pages that contain the exact phrase *bioenergy center*. Figure A-12 compares the two-word searches with the phrase search. Figure A-13 illustrates your phrase search results.

7. **Use the same table to record your results, then save your document**

> ### QUICK TIP
> Be creative and try variations in your searches, especially when using a search engine for the first time. You can discover a great deal about how the search engine functions by experimenting and then recording the number and quality of your results.

> ### QUICK TIP
> Even though a phrase search returns far fewer results than a two-word search, your first results might be the same, depending on the search tool's algorithms.

Other ways to search using phrases

Most search engines allow phrase searching, but not all in the same way. Most use quotation marks around words to indicate a phrase. However, some might automatically assume you are looking for a phrase when you enter two words in the Search text box, in which case quotation marks are redundant, but harmless. Some search engines might provide a drop-down menu or check box with an option for "exact phrase." Others might include an additional Search text box labeled "with this exact phrase." Sometimes the option for a phrase search might appear on an advanced search page. Use the Help or Search Tip pages at each search engine to learn how it uses and interprets phrase searching.

FIGURE A-11: Google two-keyword search results

Your two-keyword search

Your results

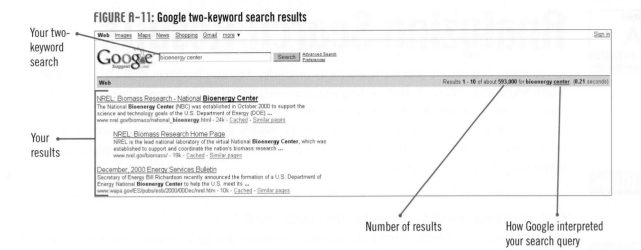

Number of results

How Google interpreted your search query

FIGURE A-12: Comparing two-word searches with a phrase search

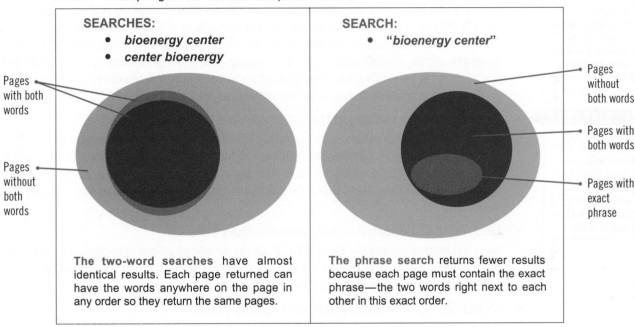

SEARCHES:
- *bioenergy center*
- *center bioenergy*

SEARCH:
- *"bioenergy center"*

Pages with both words

Pages without both words

Pages without both words

Pages with both words

Pages with exact phrase

The two-word searches have almost identical results. Each page returned can have the words anywhere on the page in any order so they return the same pages.

The phrase search returns fewer results because each page must contain the exact phrase—the two words right next to each other in this exact order.

FIGURE A-13: Google phrase search results

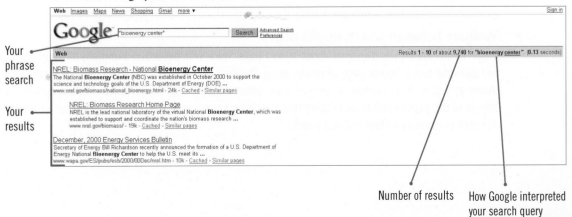

Your phrase search

Your results

Number of results

How Google interpreted your search query

Internet Research

Analyzing Search Results

As you search, you need to scan the results pages to identify Web sites that seem most likely to be useful. Search results pages offer clues that can help you zero in on the best results. Knowing how to navigate and read the results page can save you time as you select from your search results. Figure A-14 points out how to note many of the following examples in your results. ▰▰▰ Bob has conducted a search on the keyword *geothermal*. He sits down with you to analyze the search results and uses the following guidelines in determining the quality of the results.

DETAILS

- **Locate your search terms within the search result**

  Search engines often display snippets of text from the pages containing your keywords. The number of times your keywords show up in the snippet might indicate the relevance of the Web page to your search. The proximity of the words can also indicate relevance, as would a keyword in the URL. Google displays your search terms in bold for easy scanning.

- **Decipher the URL**

  The name of a URL is often **mnemonic;** that is, it indicates what the Web site is about so that its URL is easier to remember. If the URL contains one of your keywords, it is likely to be mainly about your topic. The end of the domain name (.com, .edu, .jp, .uk, and so on) indicates either a certain type of Web site or its geographic domain. If a URL ends in .gov, it is a page sponsored by a government agency. If a URL ends in .uk, it is from the United Kingdom. Being aware of this as you scan your results can be very helpful. A search for *domain names* or *country domains* results in lists you can check URLs against.

- **Note the result's ranking in the list of possible Web pages**

  Search engines use **algorithms**, or mathematical formulas, to rank each Web site according to the terms used in your search query. Every search engine has a slightly different algorithm for figuring out which is the "best" Web site, but all place their best picks at the top of the list. Generally speaking, you shouldn't have to go through more than several pages of search results to find several useful pages. If you do, try refining your search.

- **Determine if the search engine uses directory links**

  More and more search engines are creating directories (or subject guides) of recommended Web sites on many subjects. If a search engine site has included a Web page in its directory, it might indicate relevance. Clicking a directory link sends you directly to that category of Web pages.

- **Determine if the search engine uses cached pages**

  Sometimes links to Web pages break. Search engines might not become aware of the problem until their spiders search that part of the Web again. As a result, sometimes when you click a link you get a computer error message. Google has many **cached**, or hidden, copies of indexed Web pages. If you click the word "Cached," you see the copy of the Web page with your keyword(s) highlighted, as shown in Figure A-15. Cached pages can help you find the newer or renamed or relocated version of the page, or find authors' names or other specific terms. Try a new search query using those terms to look for a new location for this site.

- **Navigate between search results pages**

  Search results are usually displayed about 10 to a page. Some searches return hundreds of pages. At Google you navigate to a different page of results using the links located at the bottom of each results page, as shown in Figure A-16. Google, as well as some other engines, also offers search-refining options at the bottom of the page of results. Remember that the better your search strategy, the fewer pages of results you will need to examine to find relevant pages.

FIGURE A-14: Top of Google search results page

Your search

.org and .com indicate the kind of site and content

Cached page available

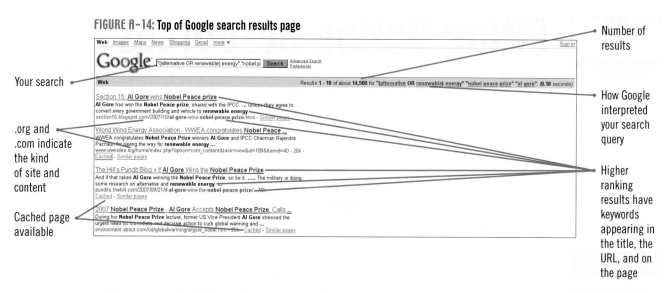

Number of results

How Google interpreted your search query

Higher ranking results have keywords appearing in the title, the URL, and on the page

FIGURE A-15: Google's cache of a page from World Wind Energy Association

Google's notification that this is a cached page

Your search and how your keywords or phrases will be highlighted on the cached page

Google's image of the Web page taken previously and cached

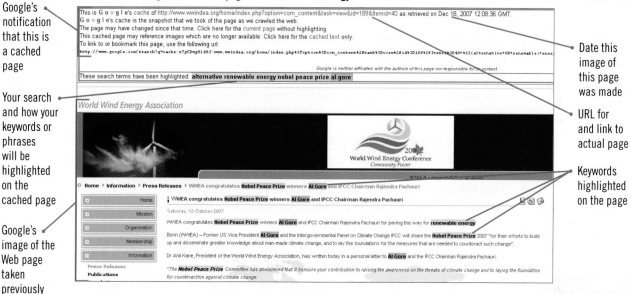

Date this image of this page was made

URL for and link to actual page

Keywords highlighted on the page

FIGURE A-16: Bottom of a Google search results page

More pages of search results *(Best results should be on the first few pages if you have created a good search strategy)*

Option to search within these results to narrow search

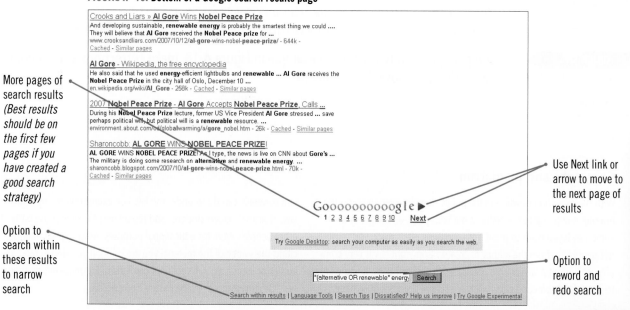

Use Next link or arrow to move to the next page of results

Option to reword and redo search

Citing Online Resources

When you use information from Web pages for classwork, you need to list them in your works cited. Even if your research is not for school, it is a good idea to gather enough information about each Web page so that you, or someone reading your work, can find it later. To present the relevant data about each site consistently, use a recognized citation format. **Citation formats** are style guides that standardize how citations are written. Two widely accepted citation formats are those of the Modern Language Association (MLA) and the American Psychological Association (APA). These style guides provide formats for all kinds of Internet information. For academic work, always check with your instructor to see which style guide format is preferred. See Table A-3 for citation tips. Bob advises you to use the MLA format to record citations for the Web pages you are finding in a way that will make your list consistent and easy for you or your colleagues to find again.

STEPS

QUICK TIP

To learn more, go to the Online Companion at www.course.com/ illustrated/research4 for citation guide links, under "Other resources."

1. **Review Figure A-17, which shows the elements of an MLA citation format**

   Figure A-18 shows an example MLA citation, and Figure A-19 shows part of the Web page cited in the example.

2. **Locate the author named in Figure A-19, then type the name in the Citing Online Resources table in your document**

   MLA format for author names is surname (last name) first, followed by a comma, then the personal name (first name) followed by a period. Note that many Web pages do not display this information as clearly as the example. You might have to look to find it and it might not be provided at all.

3. **Locate the title of the Web page in Figure A-19 and type it in the same table**

   MLA format requires quotation marks around the title with a period at the end of the title.

4. **Find the title of the Web site and type it in the same table**

   MLA format requires the title be underlined and followed by a period.

5. **Look for the date the Web page was created or the date it was last updated**

   As in this example, sometimes there is no creation/update date and you must skip this step.

QUICK TIP

The URL for any Web page is visible in the browser's address bar, but is not shown in Figure A-19.

6. **Type http://science.howstuffworks.com/solar-cell.htm in the same table in your document**

   The URL (Internet address) should be enclosed in angle brackets < > and should not be underlined.

7. **Type the date that you view this Web page in the same table**

   MLA format for dates is *DD Month Abbreviation YYYY* followed by a period. For example: 15 Oct. 2008. It is important to record the date you view a Web page because pages are changed frequently.

QUICK TIP

Be sure to use all of the required punctuation.

8. **Compare your citation with the example in Figure A-18, make corrections as needed, then save, print, and close the document**

Copyright and plagiarism

With the exception of works in the public domain, everything on the Internet is copyrighted, whether it is a Web page, an image, or an audio file. If you want to profit from someone else's work, you must get permission from the author or creator. Copyright law is very complex, so consult a lawyer who specializes in copyright law. If you want to use part of someone else's work in a school assignment or paper, you generally can do so under the Fair Use exemption to copyright law. "Fair use" allows students and researchers to copy or use parts of other people's work for educational purposes. Always give credit by citing the source of the material you are using. If you don't credit an author or source, you are guilty of plagiarism. For more information, see "Other resources" in the Online Companion.

FIGURE A-17: MLA citation style format for a Web page

Author Last Name, Author First Name.
"Web Page Title."
Web Site Title.
Date site created or revised.
<Full Internet address>
Date you viewed the Web page.

FIGURE A-18: MLA citation format for Web page below in Figure A-19

Aldous, Scott.
"How Solar Cells Work."
Howstuffworks.
<http://science.howstuffworks.com/solar-cell.htm>
15 Oct. 2008.

FIGURE A-19: Howstuffworks page cited above in Figure-A-18

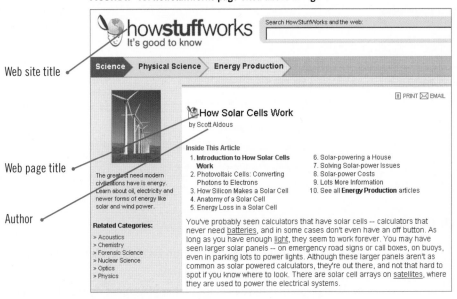

TABLE A-3: Citation tips

citation section	tips
Author	• When authors aren't named, skip this section • If a corporate author is named, such as an association, institution, or government agency, use it in the author section
Page title	• Sometimes the title is not clear; it might be under a banner or logo at the top of the page • If you are citing the whole Web site, you can skip this section, which is for a specific page
URL	• The URL should not be underlined • Some word processors automatically underline URLs, so you might need to remove the underline
Date created/revised	• Sometimes a date can be difficult to find; it might be at the very bottom of the page • When dates aren't provided, skip this section
Date viewed	• If you print the page, the date is at the lower-right corner of your printout • If you are not printing, note the date for your citation

Practice

▼ CONCEPTS REVIEW

Label each element of Figure A-20.

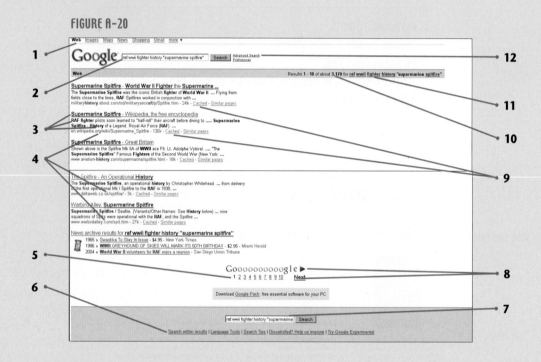

FIGURE A-20

Match each term with the statement that best describes it.

13. **Result's ranking**
14. **Cached page**
15. **Search engine**
16. **Keywords**
17. **Sponsored links**
18. **Search tools**
19. **Synonyms**

a. A Web site that locates information on the Internet by searching Web pages
b. Words that describe your search topic
c. Web pages that have paid for higher placement on search result pages
d. The order in which a search tool returns results, usually based on relevancy
e. A copy of a Web page stored by a search engine
f. Words that have similar meanings
g. Services that find information on the Internet and the Web

Select the best answer from the list of choices.

20. Which is *not* a step in the recommended Internet research strategy?
   a. Defining your research topic
   b. Choosing the proper Internet search tool
   c. Entering keywords without preparation
   d. Evaluating your search results

21. Phrase searching helps you find:

    a. Words in the order you specify.

    b. Keywords.

    c. Wildcards.

    d. Synonyms.

22. Which is *not* part of an MLA citation for a generic Web page?

    a. Author's first name

    b. Web page title

    c. City from which Web page is published

    d. URL

23. Where is it best to put the most important keyword in your search?

    a. Anywhere in your search query

    b. At the beginning of your search query

    c. At the end of your search query

    d. The order of the keywords does not make any difference.

▼ SKILLS REVIEW

1. Understand Internet search tools.

    a. Open the file IR A-2.doc from the drive and folder where you store your Data Files, save it as **Internet Searches** where you are saving files for this book, then type your name in the space provided.

    b. In the Skill #1 box in your document, write a paragraph describing the four common Internet search tools.

    c. Save your document.

2. Create an Internet research strategy.

    a. In the Skill #2 table in your document, type the seven steps of an effective Internet research strategy in order.

    b. Write a paragraph below the steps explaining the importance of translating your topic into a search query and the value of refining your query to retrieve better results, then save your document.

3. Identify the right keywords.

    a. You have defined your search topic as follows: I want to find information about the history of cotton farming.

    b. Type the topic in the Skill #3 table in your document.

    c. Boldface or underline the three keywords in the topic and list them below the topic.

    d. Think of at least three synonyms or related words for the keywords (they might all be for the same keyword).

    e. Type the synonyms and related words next to the appropriate keywords in your document, then save your document.

4. Perform a basic search.

    a. You have decided to search for **cotton plantations**.

    b. Go to the Online Companion at www.course.com/illustrated/research4, then click the Google link.

    c. Perform the search **cotton plantations**, record the total number of results in the Skill #4 table in your document, then save it.

5. Add keywords.

    a. You need information about museums covering cotton plantations and gins.

    b. Go to the Online Companion, then click the Google link.

    c. Perform the search **cotton plantation**, examine the results only on the first page of results, and record the number that seem relevant to your needs in the Skill #5 table in your document.

    d. Add the keyword **gin**, perform this search, and in the same table record the number of relevant results that appear on your first page of results.

    e. Add the keyword **museum**, perform this search, in the same table record the number of relevant results that appear on your first page of results, as shown in Figure A-21, then save your document.

FIGURE A-21

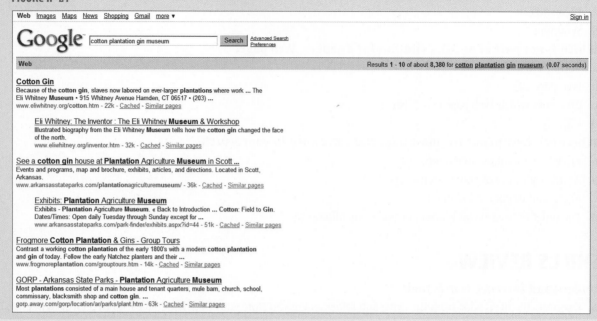

6. Phrase search.
a. Go to the Online Companion, then click the Google link.

b. Search for the phrase **"cotton plantations"**.

c. Use the Skill #6 table in your document to record the number of search results, then save your document.

7. Analyze search results.
a. Go to the Online Companion, then click the Google link.

b. Search for **cotton**, then record the total number of results in the Skill #7 table in your document.

c. In the same table, record the number of results on the first page of results that contain your keyword in the URL.

d. Record the number of results that you know have paid to be listed on the first page of results.

e. Record the number of results on the first page of results that Google has cached.

f. Record whether Google displays your search term in bold in each result, then save your document.

8. Cite online resources.
a. Select one of the Web pages returned by one of your cotton-related searches.

b. Print the page you plan to cite, then write your name at the top of the page.

c. In the Skill #8 box, create an MLA format citation for the page.

d. Save, print, and close your document, then exit your word-processing program.

▼ INDEPENDENT CHALLENGE 1

You want to find information on George Harrison's use of the sitar in the song "Norwegian Wood." You decide to use phrase searching to narrow your search results.

a. Start a new document in your word processor, type your name at the top, then save it as **Harrison** where you are saving files for this book.

b. Go to the Online Companion at www.course.com/illustrated/research4, then click the Google link.

c. Perform the search **george harrison**, then record the number of results in your document.

d. Perform the search **norwegian wood**, then record the number of results in your document.

e. Perform the search **george harrison norwegian wood**, then record the number of results in your document.

f. Perform the phrase search **"george harrison" "norwegian wood"**, then record the number of results in your document.

g. In your document, type a few sentences describing your results and explaining why the last search found fewer results.

Advanced Challenge Exercise

- Perform the search **"George Harrison" sitar**, then record the number of results in your document.
- Perform the search **"George Harrison" sitar "World Music"**, then record the number of results in your document.
- Perform the search **"George Harrison" sitar "World Music" audio**, then record the number of results, as shown in Figure A-22, in your document.
- Record the number of results appearing on the first page of search results.
- Record the number of results on the first page of results that contain one of your keywords or keyword phrases in the title.
- Record the number of results on your first page of results that are from the domain .uk.
- Record the first part of the URL of any result on your first page of results that mentions an audio clip in the description.

h. Save your document, print it, close it, then exit your word-processing program.

FIGURE A-22

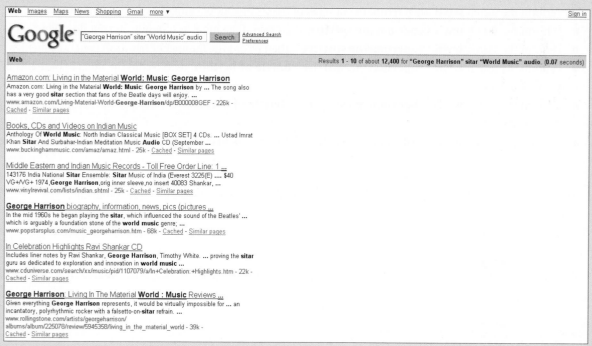

▼ INDEPENDENT CHALLENGE 2

Your friend is considering a career change and wants you to help with a Web search. The topic statement is: I want to find information about careers in computing in Great Britain.

a. Start a new document in your word processor, save it as **UK Computing** where you are saving files for this book, then type the topic statement at the top of the page.

b. Boldface or underline the keywords in the topic.

c. Copy each keyword onto a separate line.

d. Adjacent to each keyword, type relevant synonyms and related words.

e. From all of your keywords, compose a search and type it on the next line (include one phrase in the search).

f. Go to the Online Companion at www.course.com/illustrated/research4, then click the Yahoo! link.

g. Perform your search, then record the number of search results in your file.

h. Add your name to the document, save it, print it, close it, then exit your word-processing program.

▼ INDEPENDENT CHALLENGE 3

You want to search the Internet for information on a topic of your choosing.

a. Create a new document in your word-processing program, save it as **My Topic** where you are saving files for this book, and add your name to the top.

b. Decide on a topic and describe it in a sentence in your document.

c. Note your keywords and any synonyms or related terms in your document.

d. Develop a basic search query, choose a search engine, and perform a search.

e. Analyze the search results using the skills you learned in this unit.

f. Print the first page of results, then write your name at the top of the page.

g. In the document, briefly describe how you analyzed your results.

h. Create an MLA citation for one of your resulting pages in your document, then save the document.

Advanced Challenge Exercise

- Perform the search **wwii**, then record the number of results in your document.
- Perform the search **wwii supermarine spitfire**, then record the number of results in your document.
- Perform the search **wwii "supermarine spitfire"**, then record the number of results in your document.
- Perform the search **wwii "supermarine spitfire" battle of britain**, then record the number of results in your document.
- Perform the search **wwii "supermarine spitfire" "battle of britain"** then record the number of results in your document.
- Perform the search **wwii "supermarine spitfire" "battle of britain" "september 15"**, then record the number of results, as shown in Figure A-23, in your document.

i. Add your name to the document, save, print, and close it, then exit your word-processing program.

FIGURE A-23

▼ REAL LIFE INDEPENDENT CHALLENGE

In today's job market, many people find that technical skills, while necessary, are not sufficient for career advancement. Employability skills are equally important to maintaining a job and improving one's position. You decide to research how to improve your employability skills.

a. Start a new document in your word processor, record your name at the top, then save it as **Employability** where you are saving files for this book.

b. Use the Online Companion (www.course.com/illustrated/rsearch4) to go to Google.

c. Click in the Search text box, enter **employability**, then click Google Search.

d. Scroll down and look at the search results. You notice that these results contain links not directly related to employability skills. To refine your search, add another keyword.

e. Go to Google, modify your search so it reads **employability skills**, then search again.

f. Examine the search results and note they are more relevant. However, you want to know how to improve these skills, so add another keyword.

g. Modify your search so it reads **improving employability skills**, then search again.

h. Examine the search results and note how many more pertain directly to improving employability skills. You can refine your search even further by using quotation marks to perform a phrase search.

i. Modify your search so it reads **"improving employability skills"**, then search again.

j. Explore the search results, as shown in Figure A-24.

k. Choose an article, read it, write a summary of the article's information on how to improve your employability skills, record your name at the top, then print your document.

FIGURE A-24

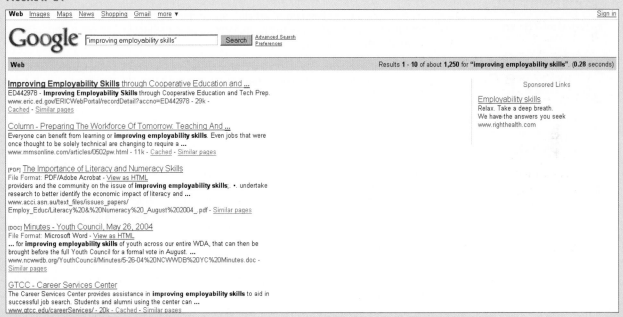

▼ VISUAL WORKSHOP

A friend gives you a printout of the Web page shown in Figure A-25, but the URL that should be at the bottom of the page is torn off. You decide to find the page from the information on the printout. Using a search engine of your choice, search for the page. Create a new document in your word-processing program, then save it as **Hockey** where you are saving files for this book. Record the citation for this Web page in MLA format. Save, print, and close the document, then exit your word-processing program.

FIGURE A-25

Constructing Complex Searches

Files You Will Need:

IR B-1.doc

IR B-2.doc

Many search engines allow **complex search queries,** or advanced searches, which use special connecting words and symbols called Boolean operators. Boolean operators define the relationships between keywords or phrases in a search. They instruct the search engine how to interpret your search and expand, narrow, or restrict your search results. Search filters provide another method to narrow your search by limiting its scope to a specific part of the Web. Combining complex queries with search filters lets you focus more exactly on the information you need. You can also use metasearch engines to simultaneously search the indexes of multiple search engines. The city planning team requests information on alternative energy-related associations in the region and on alternative energy use in surrounding states and provinces. To help you design search strategies, Bob, your friend the reference librarian, provides information on Boolean operators and filters to help refine your searches.

OBJECTIVES

Understand Boolean operators

Narrow a search with the
   AND operator

Expand a search with the
   OR operator

Restrict a search with the AND
   NOT operator

Use multiple Boolean operators

Search with filters

Combine Boolean operators
   and filters

Use metasearch engines

Understanding Boolean Operators

The English language uses **syntax**, a special set of rules, for combining words to form grammatical sentences. Search engines use **Boolean logic**, a special mathematical syntax, to perform complex searches. In Boolean logic, keywords act like nouns in a sentence. Like nouns, keywords represent subjects. You use **Boolean operators**, connecting words such as AND, OR, and AND NOT, to tell a search engine how to interpret your complex searches. Boolean operators work like conjunctions in a sentence, defining connections between keywords. Boolean logic is usually illustrated with Venn diagrams. ⬛⬛⬛ Bob provides information on Boolean operators and on Venn diagrams, which illustrate how the operators work. He explains that you can create more efficient complex searches when you understand how Boolean operators connect keywords.

DETAILS

To review Boolean operators and Venn diagrams:

QUICK TIP

If you have trouble deciding which Boolean operator to use in your search strategy, sketch a Venn diagram labeled with your terms and it will become clear.

- **Venn diagrams**

  Venn diagrams are drawings that visually represent searches using Boolean operators. For example, consider the Venn diagrams in Figure B-1. The rectangle represents the World Wide Web. Circles inside the rectangle represent groups of related Web pages, called **sets**. One circle represents a search for pages containing the word *cats*. Another circle represents a search for *dogs*. If the circles overlap, the overlapping area represents pages that are retrieved by both searches. This overlapping area is called the **intersection** of the sets. If you limit your search to pages containing *both* the words, the search results are represented by the intersection of these two circles. If you expand your search to pages containing *either* word, the search results are represented by both full circles. This is called the **union** of the two sets. If you restrict your search to pages containing one word, but *not* the other one, this search is represented by the part of one circle that does *not* overlap the other one. This search excludes one set from the other. Table B-1 shows how the searches illustrated by the Venn diagrams are entered and interpreted.

QUICK TIP

Always use CAPITAL LETTERS when typing any Boolean operator. If you type the word *and* in lowercase, it will either be interpreted as a keyword or ignored as a stop word.

- **Boolean operators**

  Boolean operators, **AND**, **OR**, and **AND NOT**, expand, narrow, or restrict searches based on Boolean logic. Boolean logic, or Boolean algebra, is the field of mathematics that defines how Boolean operators manipulate large sets of data. Search engines handle large data sets and use Boolean logic to perform complex searches, usually called advanced searches. Boolean operators act as commands to the search engine. How they connect keywords and phrases tells the search engine how to interpret your search and thus helps you retrieve the results you want. Boolean operators control which keywords *must* be on the Web page (AND), which *may or may not* be on the Web page (OR), and which keyword *must not* be on the Web page (AND NOT).

QUICK TIP

If you're unsure about using Boolean operators at a new search engine or unsure about its default operator, refer to the Help pages.

- **Default Boolean operator**

  Search engines insert Boolean operators into multiple word searches whether you supply them in the search query or not. The operator that the engine automatically uses is called the **default operator**. Most search engines default to AND. Others default to OR. When you search two or more words, some engines assume you want the words in a phrase and treat the query as if you used quotation marks. Being aware of an engine's default operator is important to create the best search strategy for that engine.

- **Where to use Boolean operators**

  Some search engines allow Boolean searching on the basic search page, but some allow it only on the advanced search page. In the past, almost all search engines recognized all Boolean operators when typed in all capital letters in the Search text box on the basic search page. Now many only recognize them if you use the advanced search page's specialized text boxes. Some do not allow the use of the English words AND or NOT, but do allow the plus sign (+) or minus sign (−) instead.

Constructing Complex Searches

FIGURE B-1: Venn diagrams comparing search results for six searches

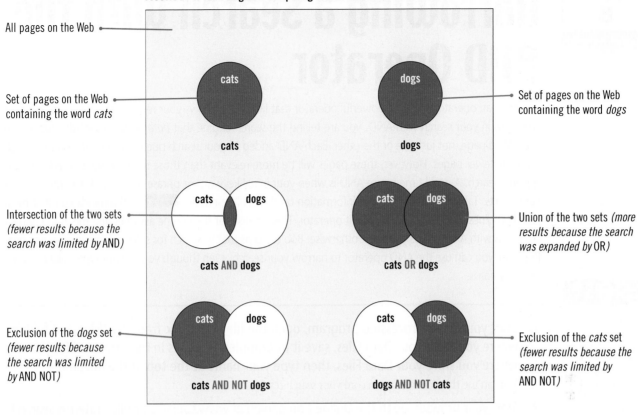

All pages on the Web

Set of pages on the Web containing the word *cats*

Set of pages on the Web containing the word *dogs*

Intersection of the two sets *(fewer results because the search was limited by* AND *)*

Union of the two sets *(more results because the search was expanded by* OR *)*

Exclusion of the *dogs* set *(fewer results because the search was limited by* AND NOT *)*

Exclusion of the *cats* set *(fewer results because the search was limited by* AND NOT *)*

cats

dogs

cats AND dogs

cats OR dogs

cats AND NOT dogs

dogs AND NOT cats

TABLE B-1: How the searches represented in Figure B-1 might be entered in and interpreted by a search tool

search	operator	search interpreted as asking for
cats	-	Web pages containing the word *cats*
dogs	-	Web pages containing the word *dogs*
cats dogs	**AND**	Web pages containing <u>both</u> words (AND is the assumed operator in most search tools so you rarely type it)
cats OR dogs	**OR**	Web pages containing <u>either</u> word
cats -dogs	**AND NOT**	Web pages containing the word *cats* but <u>not</u> the word *dogs*
dogs -cats	**AND NOT**	Web pages containing the word *dogs* but <u>not</u> the word *cats*

Remembering Boolean logic

You might remember Boolean logic and Venn diagrams from a math class. George Boole (1815–1864), an Englishman, invented a form of symbolic logic called Boolean algebra, which is used in the fields of mathematics, logic, computer science, and artificial intelligence. John Venn (1843–1923), also an Englishman, used his diagrams to explain visually what Boole had described symbolically—the intersection, union, and exclusion of sets. Little did they know then that they were creating the foundation of the language that Internet search engines use today.

Narrowing a Search with the AND Operator

The Boolean operator AND is a powerful operator that limits or narrows your results. Whenever you connect keywords in your search with AND, you are telling the search engine that *both* of the keywords must be on every Web page, not just one or the other. Each AND added to your search query further narrows the search results to fewer pages. However, these pages will be more relevant than those returned by a broader, or less specific, search. A good time to use AND is when your initial keyword or phrase search finds too many irrelevant results. Table B-2 provides more information on the AND operator. ░▒▓░ Bob reminds you that most search engines use AND as their default operator. This means that the engine assumes you mean to connect keywords with AND unless you tell it otherwise. Bob explains that to search for solar energy associations near Portland, you can use the AND operator to narrow your search, even though you will not type AND between your keywords.

STEPS

1. **Start your word-processing program, open the file IR B-1.doc from the drive and folder where you store your Data Files, save it as Complex Searches in the drive and folder where you store your Data Files, then type your name at the top of the document**

   You can use this document to record your search results.

2. **Start your browser, go to the Online Companion at www.course.com/illustrated/research4, then click the Google link (under "Search engines")**

   The Google Basic Search page opens.

QUICK TIP

Don't forget the quotation marks, which show that you want your keywords searched as a phrase.

3. **Type "solar energy association" in the Search text box, then click Google Search**

4. **Use the Narrowing a Search with the AND Operator table in your document to record the number of search results**

   Noting the number of results illustrates how Boolean operators can broaden or narrow a search.

QUICK TIP

You can but do not have to capitalize proper names in search text boxes.

5. **Delete the first search in the Search text box, type portland, then click Google Search**

6. **Record the number of search results in the same table in your document**

   To find the pages that contain *both* the name *Portland* and the phrase "*solar energy association*," you would have to read as many Web pages as these two resulting sets combined. But you realize you can create a search strategy using a Boolean operator to identify these pages for you.

QUICK TIP

If you were to add a third keyword with the AND operator, you would get *fewer* results because AND always limits or narrows your search. So, fewer results are returned for the search: "solar energy association" AND "Portland" AND "passive solar."

7. **Delete the search in the Search text box, type "solar energy association" portland, then click Search**

   This search, using the assumed AND operator, narrows your results to *solar energy association* pages that also contain *Portland*. Figure B-2 is a diagram of this search. Figure B-3 illustrates the search results. This search is meant to make you aware of how the Boolean operator AND affects your results, even when you don't enter it. Because most search engines use AND as the default operator now, you rarely need to enter it. Instead, you just enter your keywords and the ANDs are assumed.

8. **Record the number of search results in your document, then save the document**

Keeping a search diary

Boolean search statements provide a standardized way of noting your searches. It is a good idea to log searches as you perform them, noting the Boolean operators. This helps you remember what searches you have tried and which ones yielded useful results. Your search logs can also be used by others to reproduce your search results.

FIGURE B-2: Venn diagram illustrating results for: "solar energy association" AND portland

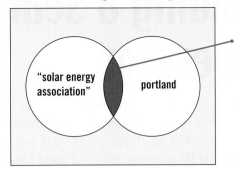

The intersection of the two sets represents your search results: Web pages containing both "solar energy association" AND portland

FIGURE B-3: Google search results: "solar energy association" AND portland

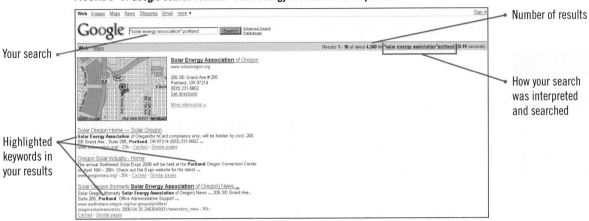

Your search

Number of results

How your search was interpreted and searched

Highlighted keywords in your results

TABLE B-2: The Boolean operator AND

why/when to use	• When finding too many irrelevant results • To narrow, limit, or focus a search • To force the search of a stop word
variations	• Usually unnecessary because most search engines assume AND • AND • + (the plus sign)
searches	• Most basic searches allow either + or AND, but its use is not required • Most advanced searches provide a specialized text box (or check box or list box) often labeled "with all of the words" or "must include"
sample uses /results	• **use:** *solar panels*; **result:** assumed AND between keywords narrows search and returns fewer results • **use:** *+and i love her*; **result:** forces inclusion of the stop word "and"

Using the plus sign: +

The plus sign is usually not required to represent the Boolean operator AND. When you enter more than one keyword, AND is assumed by most search engines. However, you still might encounter some search tools in which you have to use + or AND. You will know by checking the tool's Help page.

The plus sign is very useful to prevent a search engine from ignoring a stop word. For example, *Henry +I* produces the same results as *"Henry I."* The plus sign functions like quotation marks around a phrase. Whether using quotes or +, you are forcing the search engine to look for a word it would normally ignore.

When you use the plus sign, you must leave a space in front of it, but no space between it and the keyword it is connecting to the first keyword. Examples: *+the goal orr* (used to force inclusion of a stop word); *music +blues +memphis* (used as the Boolean AND).

Expanding a Search with the OR Operator

As you have seen, the AND Boolean operator *narrows* your search. Conversely, the Boolean operator OR *expands* or broadens your results. When you connect keywords in your search with OR, you are telling the search engine to list every Web page that contains any of the keywords. In other words, every page returned must have at least one of the keywords on it but it doesn't need to have more than one. Each OR added to your search expands the search to include more Web pages. A good time to use OR is when your initial search finds too few results. Refer to the synonyms or related words you identified when developing your search strategy and connect one or more to your search with OR. Table B-3 provides more information about the OR operator. ■■■■ The city planning team requests that you find information on wind energy. Checking your list of synonyms and related words, you decide to perform a complex search using OR to connect the keyword phrases "renewable energy" and "alternative energy."

STEPS

TROUBLE
If your browser is not at Google, go to the Online Companion at www.course.com/illustrated/research4, then click the Google link.

1. **Clear the Google Search text box**

2. **In the Search text box, type "renewable energy", then click Search**

3. **Use the Expanding a Search with the OR Operator table in your document to record the number of search results**

4. **Clear the Search text box, type "alternative energy", then click Search**

5. **Use the same table in your document to record the number of search results**

6. **Clear the Search text box, type "renewable energy" "alternative energy", then click Search**

   This search requires that every page returned contains both phrases. Although you did not type it in, the search engine interpreted your search as if you had connected your phrases with the AND operator. Now you want to connect the phrases with the OR operator to expand your results.

7. **Use the same table in your document to record the number of search results**

QUICK TIP
If you were to add a third keyword with the OR operator, you would get more results, because OR always expands or broadens your search. So, even more results are returned for the search: "renewable energy" OR "alternative energy" OR "sustainable energy."

8. **Edit the Search text box so it reads "renewable energy" OR "alternative energy", then click Search**

   Figure B-4 illustrates your search results with a Venn diagram. This search only requires that every page returned contains one of your phrases, but not necessarily both. Figure B-5 illustrates your search results page. Numbers of results change all the time, so your results will never match the number in the figure. You might reasonably expect the number of results to equal the sum of your first two searches. But this is rarely the case because some Web pages contain both phrases and the results page eliminates many duplicates. This search is meant to make you aware of how using the Boolean operator OR affects your results.

9. **Record the number of search results in your document, then save your document**

FIGURE B-4: Venn diagram illustrating results

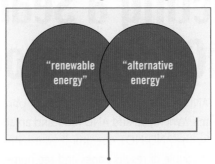

The union of the two sets represents your results: Web pages containing either "renewable energy" or "alternative energy"

FIGURE B-5: Google search results: "renewable energy" OR "alternative energy"

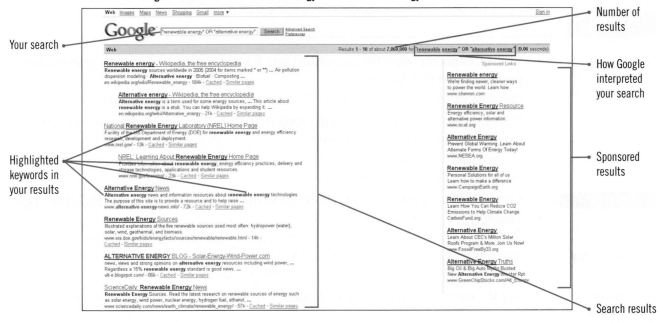

TABLE B-3: The Boolean operator OR

why/when to use	• To expand or broaden a search • To combine synonyms or related terms • When finding too few results • When you want to include more than one spelling of your keyword
searches	• Most basic searches allow OR • Most advanced searches provide a specialized text box (or check box or list box) labeled "any of the words" or "with at least one of the words"
sample use/result	• **use:** *oregon* OR *"pacific northwest"*; **result:** broadens search and returns more results • **use:** *renewable* OR *sustainable* OR *alternative*; **result:** combines synonyms and returns more results • **use:** *draft* OR *draught*; **result:** expands search to include both spellings and returns more results

Restricting a Search with the AND NOT Operator

The Boolean operator AND NOT excludes the keyword or phrase that follows it. Therefore, AND NOT narrows or limits your search. When you add AND NOT and an additional keyword to a search strategy, fewer results are returned. Use the AND NOT operator if your initial search returns too many irrelevant results. When you scan the first couple of results pages and see numerous irrelevant pages returned, try to locate any words or phrases that your desired search results should *not* contain. This is a good time to identify a category of results you do *not* want to retrieve and add it to your search with AND NOT. Table B-4 provides more information about using AND NOT. Your search results for energy associations in Portland include Web pages about both Portland, Oregon, and Portland, Maine. When you tell Bob you are only interested in Oregon, he explains the easiest way to solve this is to search the phrase "Portland Oregon." However, he suggests you practice with Boolean AND NOT logic. This way, you will not only exclude pages containing Maine, but will also see pages that contain Portland that don't contain Oregon. Before trying AND NOT, you decide to search without it to compare results.

STEPS

1. **At the Google site, clear the Search text box if necessary, type** "solar energy association" portland, **then click** Search

   The results include Web pages about both cities—Portland, Oregon, and Portland, Maine.

2. **Use the** Restricting a Search with the AND NOT Operator table **in your document to record the number of search results**

   Now you want to use AND NOT to exclude Web pages about Portland, Maine. In Google, you must use the minus sign (–) for the Boolean operator AND NOT.

QUICK TIP

If you were to add a third keyword with the AND NOT operator, you would get fewer results because AND NOT always excludes keywords or limits or narrows your search. So, fewer results are returned for the search: "solar energy association" AND NOT Maine AND NOT Oregon.

3. **Click immediately after the word** portland **in the Search text box, press [Spacebar], type** –maine, **then click** Search

   Be sure to not leave a space between the minus sign and the word *maine*. When using the minus sign (–), there must always be a space in front of it and no space between it and the next keyword. Figure B-6 shows a Venn diagram of your search. Figure B-7 illustrates your results.

4. **Use the same table to record the number of search results, then save your document**

Using the AND NOT operator

You might encounter the AND NOT Boolean operator referred to as AND NOT, ANDNOT, NOT, and most often as the minus sign (–). However it is written, the Boolean logic is the same—it excludes the following word or phrase from the search results. When you use the minus sign (–), include a space before it but do not leave a space between it and the word it is connecting to in the search query. So, a search for *cats* AND NOT *dogs* retrieves the same results as the search *cats -dogs*. Consider your search strategy before using AND NOT. If you search for *cats -dogs*, you might miss good pages that discuss both. It is a powerful tool to use with care. A search tool's Help pages should provide information about how it understands Boolean operators. Note that when you exclude a word(s) from your search results, it does not exclude them from the sponsored results.

FIGURE B-6: Venn diagram illustrating results for the search "solar energy association" AND portland AND NOT maine

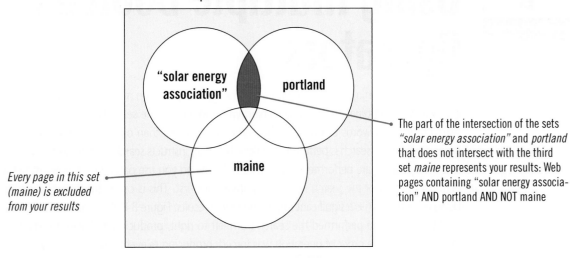

Every page in this set (maine) is excluded from your results

The part of the intersection of the sets *"solar energy association"* and *portland* that does not intersect with the third set *maine* represents your results: Web pages containing "solar energy association" AND portland AND NOT maine

FIGURE B-7: Google search "solar energy association" AND portland AND NOT maine

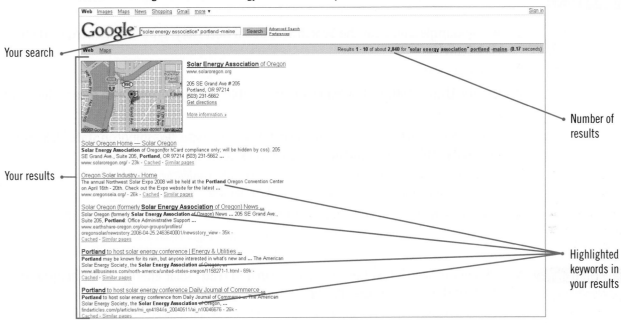

Your search

Your results

Number of results

Highlighted keywords in your results

TABLE B-4: The Boolean operator AND NOT

why/when to use	• To exclude a keyword • To limit or narrow a search • When finding too many irrelevant results • When a keyword is used in different contexts and you need to exclude one
variations	• Hyphen or minus sign (−) is the most commonly used • You might also encounter AND NOT, ANDNOT, or NOT
searches	• Most basic searches allow the minus sign (−) • Most advanced searches provide a specialized text box (or a check box or list box), labeled "must not include" or "without the words"
sample use/result	• **use:** *"alternative energy" -geothermal*; **result:** excludes *geothermal* and returns fewer results • **use:** *cardinals -"st. louis" -arizona -catholic*; **result:** excludes some nonrelevant contexts from results

Using Multiple Boolean Operators

Combining Boolean operators in your search strategy provides even more focused results. You can use operators in any logical combination. When searching with more than one set of keywords, use parentheses to tell the search tool which words belong together. When using more than one operator, use parentheses to force the order in which the search is performed. Unless the query instructs search tools to do otherwise, the query is read and the operators are performed from left to right. When you use parentheses, you instruct the search tool to perform the part of the search inside the parentheses first. This is called **forcing the order of operation**. Using parentheses has a significant impact on search results. Figure B-8 illustrates results in which the search tool read the query and performed the search from left to right, producing irrelevant results. Figure B-9 illustrates results in which the order of operation was forced, producing relevant results. See Table B-5 for steps to use in planning a complex search. ▓▓▓▓ In your last team meeting, you agreed to find information on solar energy resources from the surrounding region, not just in Portland, Oregon. Bob suggests you combine Boolean operators in a complex search. First, you want to search two sets of keywords separately so you can compare results.

STEPS

1. **At the Google site, clear the Search text box if necessary, type** "solar energy", **then click Search**

   Your results appear.

2. **Use the Using Multiple Boolean Operators table in your document to record the number of search results**

3. **Delete your previous query in the Search text box, type** "Washington state" OR "British Columbia" OR "Pacific Northwest", **then click Search**

   You learned on previous searches that if you enter only *Washington*, your results contain many pages referring to Washington, D.C., so you included the word *state*.

4. **Use the same table in your document to record the number of search results**

   Now you need to combine and limit these results to Web pages about solar energy that also refer to the Northwest, but do not refer to Oregon. You use parentheses to tell Google which sets of words belong together.

QUICK TIP

Be sure to leave no space between the minus sign and the keyword to be excluded.

5. **Click in the Search text box, edit your search to read** "solar energy" ("Washington state" OR "British Columbia" OR "Pacific Northwest") -Oregon, **then click Search**

   Remember that you must use the minus sign (–) for Google to understand you mean AND NOT. Figure B-10 illustrates your results in a Venn diagram.

6. **Use the same table in your document to record the number of search results, then save your document**

Using multiple Boolean operators in basic and advanced search forms

Most search tools contain advanced search pages, which can be convenient for putting together complex searches. If you ever find yourself unsure about what to do when using these pages, return to these basic tools: identifying keywords and related words, sketching Venn diagrams to recall how the Boolean operators work, and writing down your search strategy using the Boolean operators AND, OR, and AND NOT. Just as understanding the mathematical functions that are being performed by the calculator that you use for convenience helps you successfully exploit your calculator, understanding Boolean logic helps you create successful online search strategies when you use the convenience of advanced search pages. However, the more complicated your complex searches become, the more likely you will need to go back to the basic search page where you have more control over your search statement.

FIGURE B-8: Venn diagram illustrating the search: *constitution* AND *American* OR *"United States"*

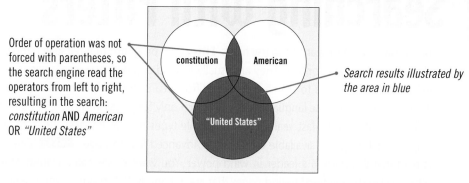

Order of operation was not forced with parentheses, so the search engine read the operators from left to right, resulting in the search: *constitution* AND *American* OR *"United States"*

Search results illustrated by the area in blue

FIGURE B-9: Venn diagram illustrating the search: *constitution* AND (*American* OR *"United States"*)

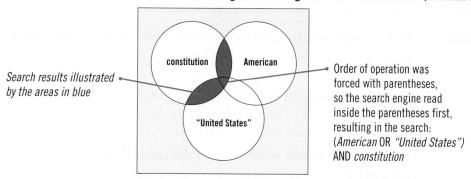

Search results illustrated by the areas in blue

Order of operation was forced with parentheses, so the search engine read inside the parentheses first, resulting in the search: (*American* OR *"United States"*) AND *constitution*

FIGURE B-10: Venn diagram illustrating the search: *"solar energy"* AND (*"Washington state"* OR *"British Columbia"* OR *"Pacific Northwest"*) AND NOT *Oregon*

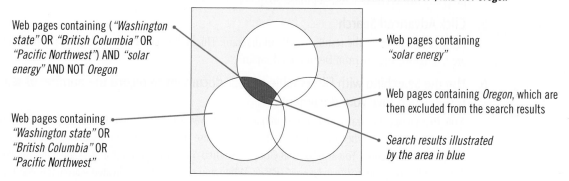

Web pages containing (*"Washington state"* OR *"British Columbia"* OR *"Pacific Northwest"*) AND *"solar energy"* AND NOT *Oregon*

Web pages containing *"Washington state"* OR *"British Columbia"* OR *"Pacific Northwest"*

Web pages containing *"solar energy"*

Web pages containing *Oregon*, which are then excluded from the search results

Search results illustrated by the area in blue

TABLE B-5: Planning a complex search

You can combine Boolean operators to develop a complex search strategy. For example: If you want to use Google to search alternative energy in British Columbia or Alberta, Canada, but do not want pages on geothermal energy, here are sample steps to develop an effective strategy:

1.	Identify the first concept. Use keywords, synonyms, and related words. Connect them with OR and surround them with parentheses.	(British Columbia OR BC OR Alberta)
2.	Identify the second concept. Use keywords, synonyms, related words. Connect them with OR and surround them with parentheses.	(Canada OR Canadian)
3.	Identify the third concept. Quotation marks identify this as a phrase.	"alternative energy"
4.	Identify the fourth concept. You want this word excluded from your results, so you use the Boolean operator AND NOT. Google uses the minus sign (–) as AND NOT.	–geothermal
5.	Connect all of your concepts into one search statement. (*Remember: the ANDs are assumed so you don't have to type them*)	(British Columbia OR BC OR Alberta) AND (Canada OR Canadian) AND "alternative energy" -geothermal

Searching with Filters

Another way to refine a search is to use filters. **Filters** are programs that tell search tools to screen out specified types of Web pages or files. They are usually located on advanced search pages. As you develop your search strategy, use filters to search only a specified area of the Web or to exclude specified areas of the Web. For example, you use language filters to search only for pages in English, or date filters to search only for pages updated in the last year, or for certain file types such as images, audio, or video. Table B-6 lists examples of filter options available on Google's Advanced Search page. ▰▰▰▰ One of your team members read that Denmark is a leader in wind power. You want to see some Danish sites, but because you don't read Danish, you need to find pages that are in English. Bob suggests you use filters on an advanced search page to focus the search. He tells you that the domain for Denmark is .dk.

STEPS

QUICK TIP

For more complex Boolean searches, it might be more efficient to use the Basic Search page. This reduces the chances of inadvertent logic errors.

1. **At the Google site, click Advanced Search, then clear the text boxes, if necessary**

   The Google Advanced Search page includes a number of convenient options to construct searches with filters and Boolean logic.

2. **Click the Language list box, then click English**

   See Figure B-11. With this filter, your search results will only include Web pages written in English. Now you want to restrict your search to the domain exclusive to Denmark.

3. **Type .dk in the Search within a site or domain text box**

   See Figure B-11. With this filter, your search results will only include Web pages from Denmark.

4. **Type wind power in the this exact wording or phrase text box**

   See Figure B-11. Quotation marks are not needed to indicate a phrase search. This specialized text box interprets any words typed here as a phrase, so quotation marks are assumed.

5. **Click Advanced Search**

   Figure B-12 illustrates the results in a Venn diagram. The Web pages returned contain the phrase *wind power*, are in English, and are from Denmark's domain.

6. **Use the Searching with Filters table in your document to record the number of search results, then save your document**

   Note that Google has translated your search as *"wind power" site:.dk*. Quotation marks show how Google interpreted the words you typed into the "with the exact phrase" text box. The *site:.dk* is how Google translated your domain filter selection. You also see that Google searched only pages in English. Google reiterates your query as Searched *English* pages for *"wind power" site:.dk*. When you perform a complicated search, it is good to check this information to determine if the filters worked the way you expected when you developed the search strategy.

TABLE B-6: Sample filters on Google's Advanced Search page

filter	what it does
Language	Limits search to pages written in a specified language (English, French, etc.)
File type	Limits search to pages in a specified format (.pdf, .xls, .doc, .ppt, etc.)
Date	Limits search to pages updated, crawled, and indexed in the past specified time period (1 day, 1 week, 1 month, 1 year, etc.)
Site or Domain	Limits search to pages only with a specified domain or within a specified site
Where keywords are	Limits search to pages containing your keywords in a specified location (URL, title, text, etc.)
Usage Rights	Limits search to pages covered by the Creative Commons license (you must still check with each page to be sure of usage rights)
Region	Limits search to pages originating from a specified region or country (not all sites have addresses that include their country)
Numeric range	Limits search to pages containing numbers in a specified range

FIGURE B-11: Boolean logic and filters on Google's Advanced Search form

Boolean AND

Phrase search

Boolean OR

Boolean AND NOT

Language filter

Domain filter

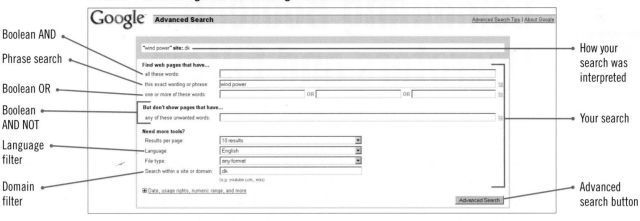

How your search was interpreted

Your search

Advanced search button

FIGURE B-12: Venn diagram illustrating results for: "wind power" AND domain:.dk AND language: English

NOT included in your results: pages containing "wind power" that are from Denmark, but that are not in English

NOT included in your results: pages containing "wind power" that are in English, but that are not from Denmark

NOT included in your results: pages in English that are from Denmark, but that do not contain "wind power"

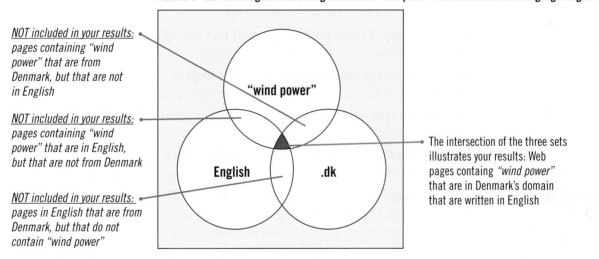

The intersection of the three sets illustrates your results: Web pages containg *"wind power"* that are in Denmark's domain that are written in English

Filtering domains in the URL

Filters search only for letters or words that appear in certain parts of a URL. The final two or three letters in the URL indicate domains. Web sites in the United States have URLs that end in three letters that represent the type of organization hosting the Web site. For example, university sites end in .edu, government sites end in .gov, commercial sites end in .com, and nonprofits end in .org. Others include .biz, .pro, .info, .net, .us, .coop, .museum, and .name. Web sites located in other countries use two-letter country codes: Canada's domain is .ca, the United Kingdom's domain is .uk, and Japan's domain is .jp. Any of these two- or three-letter codes can limit search results when using a domain filter. For a full listing of the two-letter country codes, go to www.iana.org/cctld/cctld-whois.htm. You can find other sites with this information by searching for *countries* AND *domains*.

Combining Boolean Operators and Filters

Most search tools provide advanced search pages that make entering complex searches easier. These pages allow you to combine Boolean operators and filters to create complex, very specific searches that return relevant results. See Table B-7 for an example of planning a complex search strategy. ▓▓▓▓ As discussed with your city planning team, you want to identify some university-related Canadian pages on alternative energies. You don't need pages on geothermal energy and, because they will be easy to print and share, you want pages that are in a PDF format. You are not sure how to formulate such a specific query, so you ask Bob for advice. He guides you in developing a strategy utilizing both Boolean operators and filters.

STEPS

QUICK TIP
Clear the Search text box if necessary.

1. **At the Google site, click Advanced Search, click in the all these words text box, then type university energy**
   As you saw in the last lesson, Google provides special text boxes for Boolean searching and mostly list boxes for searching with filters. This text box represents the AND Boolean operator.

2. **Click in each of the one or more of these words text box, then type one of the following words in each box: alternative sustainable renewable**
   These text boxes represent the OR Boolean operator.

3. **Click in the any of these unwanted words text box, then type geothermal**
   This text box represents the AND NOT Boolean operator.

4. **Click the Language list box arrow, then click English**
   This list box filters for Web pages written only in the language you choose.

5. **Click the File type list arrow, then click Adobe Acrobat PDF (.pdf)**
   This filters for Web pages that are only in the file format you choose.

6. **Click the Search within a site or domain list box, then type .ca**
   This filters for Web pages that are only located in the domain you specify; .ca is the domain for Canada.

QUICK TIP
Even with a fast Internet connection, you might notice that a complex search using several different operators and filters sometimes takes longer to return results.

7. **Compare your settings with those shown in Figure B-13, then click Advanced Search**
   Figure B-14 illustrates your results. Notice that near the top of the page Google restates your search. A quick check of this information verifies the Boolean text boxes and the filters worked as you expected.

8. **Use the Combining Boolean Operators and Filters table in your document to record the number of search results, then save your document**

Using the search text boxes on an advanced search page

When using advanced search text boxes, you do not actually type the Boolean operators. When using these specialized text boxes, the search engine understands the operator you want to use so you can enter multiple words without the operators. However, if you need to enter a phrase in an OR box, you need to include quotation marks around the phrase. For example, to search for *solar panels* OR *wind turbines* on Google's Advanced Search page, enter: "solar panels" and "wind turbines" in the OR text boxes. This ensures your search is interpreted as two phrases. This is an example of why, when your complex searches get more complicated, as with multiple phrases or more than three ORed keywords, it is often preferable to go back to the basic search form.

FIGURE B-13: Using Boolean logic and filters on Google's Advanced Search form

How your
search was
interpreted
by Google

Your search

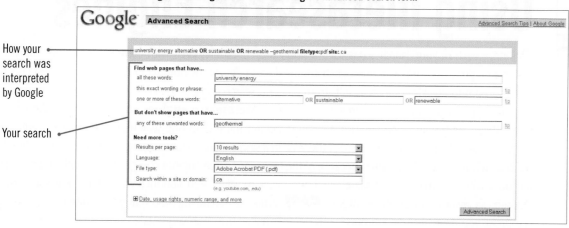

FIGURE B-14: Advanced Search results

Your search

Search
results

Number of
results

How Google
interpreted
your
advanced
search

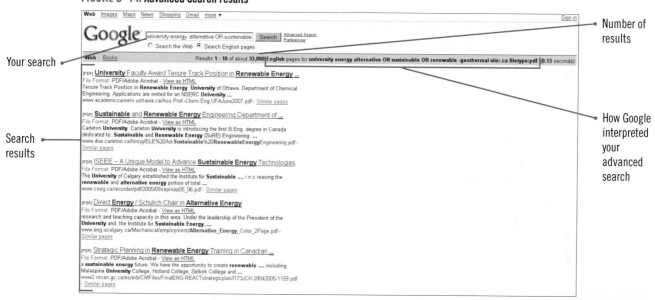

TABLE B-7: Planning a complex search using both Boolean operators and filters

You want to identify some Canadian domain pages, in PDF format, on alternative energies other than geothermal. To use Google for this search, here are the steps to develop your strategy combining Boolean operators and filters:	
1. Identify the first concept. Connect keywords with OR and surround them with parentheses.	(alternative OR renewable OR sustainable)
2. Identify the second concept. Use keywords/synonyms/related words, connect them with OR, then surround them with parentheses.	(energy OR energies)
3. Identify the third concept.	-geothermal
4. Use filters as needed.	Language: English Domain: .ca File Format: .pdf

One way to record your search strategy or enter it in the basic search text box:
    (alternative OR renewable OR sustainable) (energy OR energies) –geothermal site:.ca filetype:.pdf lang:.eng

Using Metasearch Engines

Until now, each of your searches has used a single search engine. Even with complex searching, you only search a single search engine. If one search engine doesn't deliver the number or quality of results you need, or if you want to quickly compare results from different search engines to decide which to use for a particular search, you might want to try a metasearch engine. **Metasearch engines** do not search the Web itself; rather they search search engines' indexes. By searching more than one search engine's index simultaneously, metasearch engines access more of the Web in a single search. However, metasearch engines often do not search the best search engines, because of the fees such search engines charge. Also, search engines that are busy with too many other searches at the exact moment you conduct your search are sometimes skipped, so results can be inconsistent. While searching for information on alternative energy resources, you have become intrigued with geothermal energy. Bob suggests a simple search on this topic using a metasearch engine.

STEPS

QUICK TIP

Metasearch results are broad, but often not as deep as a single search engine's. Metasearching is a good place to start when you want to check the first few results from several search engines.

1. **Go to the Online Companion at www.course.com/illustrated/research4, then click the ixquick link (under "Metasearch engines")**

2. **Click in the Search text box, then type "geothermal energy"**

   Figure B-15 illustrates your phrase search on ixquick's search form.

3. **Click Search**

   Your search is now simultaneously sent to multiple search engines. ixquick, along with Mamma.com, is one of the few "smart" metasearch engines, which translate search commands, like quotation marks, into queries that other search engines understand. If you cannot tell whether the metasearch engine you are using does this, stick with very simple searches. It might take a bit longer to return results as multiple search engines are queried.

4. **Scroll down, noting the features of the results: the ranking stars, the Highlighted Results, and the list of search engines after each result showing which engines returned each result**

   Figure B-16 illustrates the ixquick search results. Ranking stars are used to rank the results by relevance. The Highlighted Result link takes you to a copy of the Web page that highlights your keywords for easy scanning. The ixquick page also shows how each engine ranked pages and which results are sponsored.

QUICK TIP

The Highlight option provides a copy of the Web page that ixquick has at its site. It is not the original. This copy can be useful if the original site is temporarily down.

5. **Scroll down, if necessary, then click the word Highlight**

   This copy of the Web page highlights the keywords from your search query. This feature can help you quickly determine how useful the Web page might be and if you want to go to the page itself.

6. **Record the number of matching results in the Using Metasearch Engines table in your document; save, print, and close the document; then exit your word-processing program**

Maximizing metasearching

To effectively use a metasearch engine, always read its Help pages. This should let you know how "smart" the engine is in translating specific search commands into queries that other search engines understand. With this information, you know if you need to use quotation marks to indicate a phrase. If you're not sure how smart the metasearch engine is, use simple searches consisting of only a few keywords. Also, because the search engines used by a metasearch engine change regularly, note which engines are being used when you perform your search and which are returning the most useful results. Which search engines' indexes a metasearch engine searches can change often. You can usually find where one is currently searching by checking its Help pages or advanced search pages.

FIGURE B-15: ixquick search form

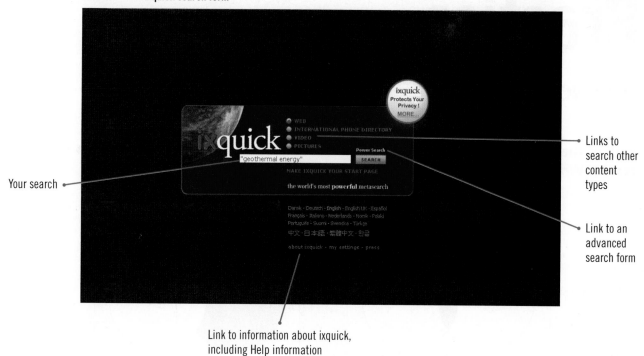

Your search

Links to
search other
content
types

Link to an
advanced
search form

Link to information about ixquick,
including Help information

FIGURE B-16: ixquick search results

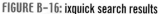
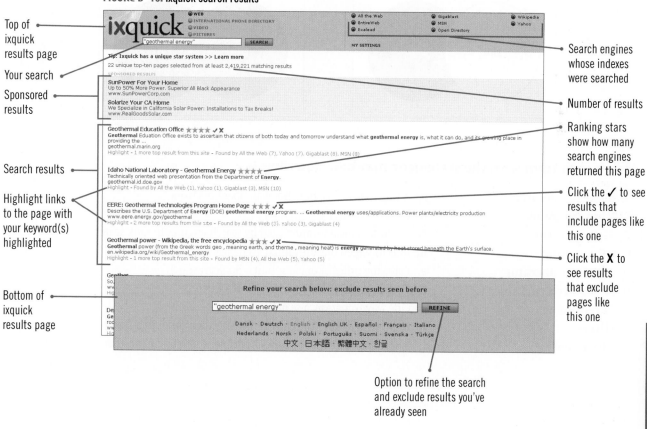

Top of
ixquick
results page

Your search

Sponsored
results

Search results

Highlight links
to the page with
your keyword(s)
highlighted

Bottom of
ixquick
results page

Search engines
whose indexes
were searched

Number of results

Ranking stars
show how many
search engines
returned this page

Click the ✓ to see
results that
include pages like
this one

Click the **X** to
see results
that exclude
pages like
this one

Option to refine the search
and exclude results you've
already seen

Practice

Each of the following Venn diagrams represents searches. The dark color represents the search results. Write out the search for each diagram.

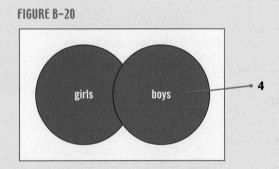

FIGURE B-17

1 — girls boys

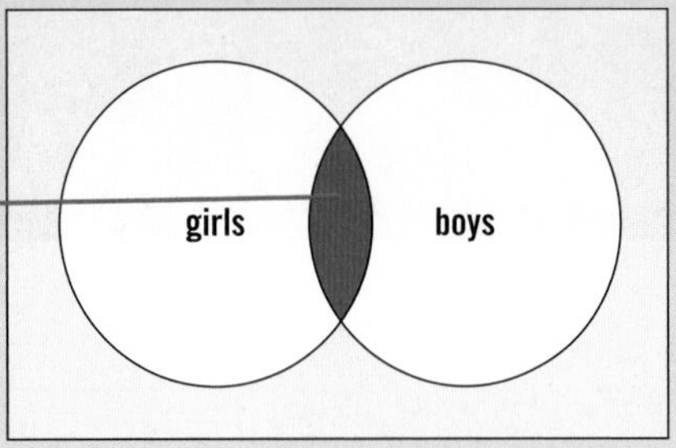

FIGURE B-19

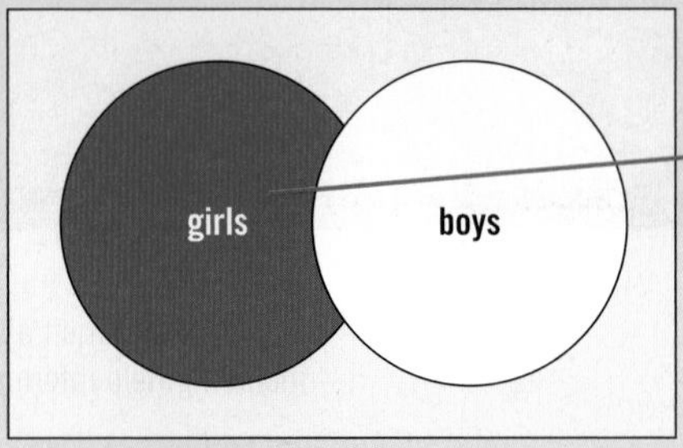

girls boys — 3

FIGURE B-18

2 — girls boys

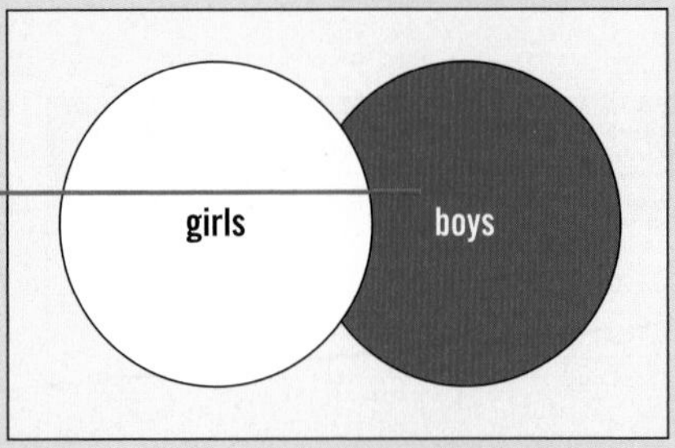

FIGURE B-20

girls boys — 4

Match each term with the statement that best describes it.

5. **Boolean operators**
6. **Venn diagrams**
7. **AND operator**
8. **OR operator**
9. **AND NOT operator**
10. **Metasearch engines**
11. **Parentheses**
12. **Filters**
13. **Algorithm**

a. A way to visualize how Boolean operators work
b. Used to connect synonyms
c. A mathematical formula used by search engines to rank search results
d. Aids to screen out unwanted Web pages
e. Force the order of operation in a Boolean search
f. Used to exclude words from a search query
g. One way to narrow a search
h. Indicate how keywords are to relate to each other in a search query
i. A search engine that searches multiple search engines rather than the Web itself

Select the best answer from the list of choices.

14. The place where two search result sets overlap is called the _____ of the two sets.
- **a.** Union
- **b.** Combination
- **c.** Intersection
- **d.** Margin

15. Each Boolean operator AND that links another keyword to your search finds:
- **a.** More Web pages.
- **b.** Exactly the same number of Web pages.
- **c.** Fewer Web pages.
- **d.** None of the above

16. Equivalent wording for the Boolean OR in an advanced search list box might be:
- **a.** Either of the words.
- **b.** All of the words.
- **c.** None of the words.
- **d.** Must not contain.

17. Which is *not* a standard variation of the Boolean operator AND NOT?
- **a.** NOT
- **b.** The hyphen or minus sign (–)
- **c.** NOT MORE
- **d.** ANDNOT

18. Which is *not* a potential downside to using metasearch engines?
- **a.** Instability
- **b.** Secrecy
- **c.** Inconsistency
- **d.** Usually limited to simple searches

19. If the order of operation in a complex Boolean search is not forced, the search tool:
- **a.** Reads the query from left to right.
- **b.** Inserts the parentheses for you.
- **c.** Returns no search results.
- **d.** Automatically applies filters to your search.

20. A search tool that doesn't recognize Boolean operators as English words in its basic search:
- **a.** Cannot be used to search with Boolean logic.
- **b.** Probably allows Boolean searching from text boxes or list boxes in its advanced search pages.
- **c.** Sometimes allows the Boolean AND and AND NOT if you use the plus sign (+) and the minus sign (–) instead of words.
- **d.** b and c

21. The part of a URL that can contain a two-letter country code is the:
- **a.** File.
- **b.** File extension.
- **c.** Domain.
- **d.** Page.

22. **Which is *not* true of all metasearch engines?**
   a. The search engines searched can change frequently.
   b. They are a good place to start when you want to see the top results from several engines.
   c. They interpret your search the way every other search engine can understand it.
   d. They might skip searching an engine they normally search if that engine is busy at that moment.

23. **Using parentheses in a complex search tells the search engine that:**
   a. The part of the search inside the parentheses should be performed first.
   b. The words inside the parentheses should be treated as a subset in the search.
   c. The words inside the parentheses should be excluded from the search.
   d. a and b

▼ SKILLS REVIEW

1. **Understand Boolean operators.**
   a. Start your word-processing program, open the file **IR B-2.doc** from the drive and folder where you store your Data Files, save it as **Boolean Searches** in the drive and folder where you store your Data Files, then add your name at the top of the page.
   b. Use the Skill #1 table in the document to describe the effects on search results of using each of the Boolean operators: AND, OR, and AND NOT.

2. **Narrow a search with the AND operator.**
   a. Start your browser, go to the Online Companion at www.course.com/illustrated/research4, then click the Google link.
   b. Perform an initial search on **baseball**.
   c. Use the Skill #2 table in your document to record the number of search results.
   d. Return to the Search page, then edit your search by adding **football**.
   e. Use the same table in your document to record the number of search results.
   f. Edit your AND search again by adding **hockey**.
   g. Use the same table in your document to record the number of search results, then save your document.

3. **Expand a search with the OR operator.**
   a. Clear the Google Search text box.
   b. Perform an initial search on **baseball**.
   c. Use the Skill #3 table in your document to record the number of search results.
   d. Return to the Search page, then edit your search by adding **OR football**.
   e. Use the Skill #3 table in your document to record the number of search results.
   f. Edit your search again by adding **OR hockey**.
   g. Use the Skill #3 table in your document to record the number of search results, then save your document.

4. **Restrict a search with the AND NOT operator.**
   a. Clear the Google Search text box.
   b. Perform an initial search on **baseball**.
   c. Use the Skill #4 table in your document to record the number of search results.
   d. Return to the Search page, then edit your search by adding **-football**.
   e. Use the same table in your document to record the number of search results.
   f. Edit your AND NOT search again by adding **-hockey**.
   g. Use the same table in your document to record the number of search results, then save your document.

5. **Use multiple Boolean operators.**
   a. Clear the Google Search text box.
   b. Perform an initial search on **football OR soccer**.
   c. Use the Skill #5 table in your document to record the number of search results.
   d. Return to the Search page, then edit your search by adding **(england OR australia)** to the initial search criteria.
   e. Use the same table in your document to record the number of search results, then save your document.

6. **Search with filters.**

   a. Clear the Google Search text box, then click Advanced Search.

   b. Perform an initial search on **football OR soccer**.

   c. Use the Skill #6 table in your document to record the number of search results.

   d. Return to the Advanced Search page, filter your previous search for Web pages written in English, then filter for pages modified and indexed in the past year, then filter the domain to only return pages with the domain for India (.in), and then perform the search.

   e. Use the same table in your document to record the number of search results, then save your document.

7. **Combine Boolean operators and filters.**

   a. Clear the Google Advanced Search text boxes and filters.

   b. In the AND Search text box, type **hockey nhl**.

   c. In the phrase Search text box, type **montreal canadiens**.

   d. Use the Skill #7 table in your document to record the number of search results.

   e. Filter the search for pages written in English, filter for pages modified and indexed in the past year, filter the domain to only return pages with the domain for Canada (.ca), as shown in Figure B-21, then perform the search.

   f. Use the same table in your document to record the number of search results, then save your document.

FIGURE B-21

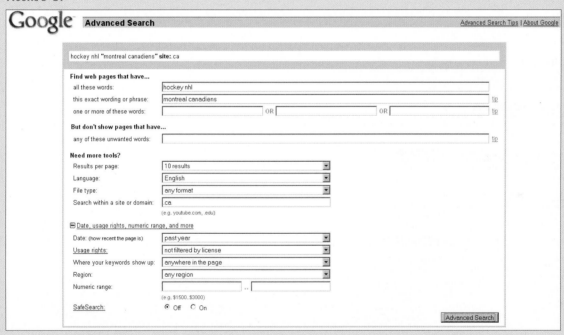

8. **Use metasearch engines.**

   a. Go to the Online Companion, click the ixquick link, then, if it is not already selected, click the WEB option button.

   b. Perform an initial search on **football**.

   c. Use the Skill #8 table in your document to record the total number of matching results.

   d. Use the same table in your document to record the number of results on the first page of results that are marked for relevancy with three or more stars.

   e. Go back to the ixquick home page, click Power Search, then fill in the search form to search for **football "world cup" (england OR australia)**.

   f. Print the search form page showing how you filled in the form, then write your name at the top of the page.

   g. Use the same table in your document to record the total number of matching results.

   h. Use the same table to record the number of results on the first page of results that are marked for relevancy with three or more stars.

   i. Save your document, print it, close it, then exit your word-processing program.

Internet Research

▼ INDEPENDENT CHALLENGE 1

You want to find Web sites in Russia (domain .ru) about the Hermitage Museum. You don't read Russian so you want the Web pages to be in English.

a. Use the Online Companion (www.course.com/illustrated/research4) to go to the Google site, then open the Google Advanced Search page.

b. Set the appropriate filters, then perform your search.

c. Print out the first page of search results, which is illustrated in Figure B-22.

d. Write your name at the top of the page.

FIGURE B-22

▼ INDEPENDENT CHALLENGE 2

Your history teacher told you that there is a connection between the Library of Congress and Thomas Jefferson. You decide to search the Internet to learn more about this connection.

a. Use the Online Companion (www.course.com/illustrated/research4) to go to the AllTheWeb search engine.

b. Click in the Search text box, then type in two appropriate search phrases using quotation marks, then perform your search.

c. Scroll through the first page of results, which is illustrated in Figure B-23, and look for a URL with the clickable phrase **more hits from** beside it.

d. Click this phrase by the link that you decide to check for your information.

e. Print out the first page of results, then write your name at the top of the page. (*Hint*: If AllTheWeb is not displaying this feature when you do your search, print out the first page of results from your original search.)

FIGURE B-23

Advanced Challenge Exercise

You are curious about the results other metasearch engines might return on your search for Thomas Jefferson and the Library of Congress.

- Use the Online Companion to go to ixquick. Click in the Search text box, enter your search phrases, then perform the search.

- Start your word processor, create a new document, save it as **Library of Congress**, record your name at the top, then record the number of results ixquick returned for your search and the search engines it searches. (*Hint*: Search engines may be listed in the upper right of your results page.)

- Use the Online Companion to go to **metacrawler**, perform the same search, then record the number of results and the search engines it searches. (*Hint*: Search engines may be listed above your results.)

- Use the Online Companion to go to **dogpile**, perform the same search, then record the number of results and the URL of top result in your document. (*Hint*: Search engines may be listed above your results.)

- Write a sentence stating which metasearch engine you liked best and why.

- Save your document and print it.

▼ INDEPENDENT CHALLENGE 3

You and some friends want to go on an ecologically friendly vacation—or an ecotour. You are interested in all North American destinations, but need the information to be in English.

a. Write your name at the top of a piece of paper, write out the topic and potential keywords, then circle the keywords and keyword phrases.

b. Write out your search strategy to make it easy to enter your query after you get online.
Hint: You should use the Language filter and the search statement should look similar to this:
keyword +("*keyword* + keyword" OR *keyword* OR *keyword* OR "*keyword* + *keyword*")

c. Use the Online Companion (www.course.com/illustrated/research4) to go to the Google Advanced Search page, then perform the search.

d. Print out a copy of the first page of your search results, then write your name at the top of the page.

e. Attach the printout to the paper on which you wrote your topic and keywords.

Advanced Challenge Exercise

While looking over the results for an ecotour in North America, you become fascinated with the idea of an ecotourism trip in either Alaska or Canada, focusing on grizzly bears or polar bears. You decide to restrict your search to find only relevant sites in English.

■ Go to the Google Basic Search page, enter your search query, then print the search page showing the query in the Search text box.

■ Perform the search, then print the first page of results. Write your name at the top of both pages.

■ Return to the Google Advanced Search page, delete your previous search, and enter your new search.

■ Print the Advanced Search page showing your search, then perform the search and print the first page of results. Write your name at the top of the page.

■ On a blank piece of paper, write a sentence or two about which search form, the basic or the advanced, you felt was easier to use for your search and why.

■ On the same page, write a sentence comparing the results of both searches.

■ Write your name at the top of this page and attach it to your printouts.

▼ REAL LIFE INDEPENDENT CHALLENGE

In our increasingly long-lived society, the number of career changes over a lifetime continues to grow. Fortunately, the Internet provides a wealth of information on how to choose a career, with everything from career-path quizzes to professional advice. You decide to avail yourself of these resources to find out how to chart a career.

a. Go to the Online Companion, then click the Google link under "Search engines."

b. In the Search text box, type **choose career**, then click Google Search. A list of pages matching your search query appears. It occurs to you that using only the keyword, "choose," limits your search results. So, you consider and list possible synonyms for the keyword "choose."

c. Go to Google and type **(choose OR pick OR select OR find) career** in the Search text box, then click Google Search. Notice that the search results contain a much wider array of possible resources for charting your career path. However, you are only interested in career advice, not career quizzes or tests, so you redesign your search strategy to exclude quizzes and tests from the search.

d. Go to Google and edit your search query to read **(choose OR pick OR select OR find) career -quiz -test** in the Search text box, then click Google Search. Note that the results no longer list career-related quizzes. Note also that your AND NOT exclusions did not apply to the sponsored results. Your results are illustrated in Figure B-24.

e. Scroll down, examine the search results, then find an article that offers information about how to choose a career. Open the article and read it.

f. Write a one- or two-paragraph summary of the article, explaining how this information can help you chart your career, then write your name at the top of the page.

FIGURE B-24

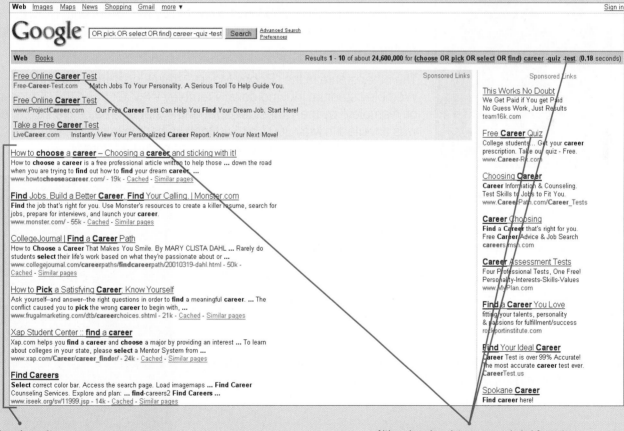

Search results

Although *quiz* and *test* were excluded from the search results, they still appear in the sponsored results, a good reminder that sponsored results are not the same as the actual search results.

▼ VISUAL WORKSHOP

The partial Web page shown in Figure B-25 concerns the captain of England's 1966 World Cup winning team. Create a complex search to find this page, using the following steps.

    a. On Google's Advanced Search page, use the following search text boxes and filters to find this page: "all these words"; "this exact wording or phrase"; Language = English; and Domain =.uk.

    b. When you find the page, print it.

    c. Print the Google Advanced Search page showing how you filled it in to find the page.

    d. Write your name at the top of both pages.

FIGURE B-25

Statues

There are two statues dedicated to Bobby Moore, both of which have been created by the noted sculptor Philip Jackson.

The first one entitled "Champions" is located at the top of Green Street not far from Upton Park. This features Geoff Hurst, Martin Peters and Ray Wilson holding Bobby Moore aloft.

Standing 5 metres high and weighing over 4 tonnes the statue is an imposing site. The finances were provided by West Ham United, The London Borough of Newham, Green Street SRB, Arts Council for England and Arts & Business.

The unveiling in April 2003 was attended by Mrs Stephanie Moore, Martin Peters, Geoff Hurst and other members of the 1966 World Cup winning team.

The other statue is the "Bobby Moore" statue located at the new Wembley stadium looking down Wembley Way. Dubbed the "Colossu of Wembley" by the Times newspaper the statue is twice life size and was unveiled in May 2007 by Sir Bobby Charlton in front of various guests including Stephanie Moore and the Prime Minister.

The statue also contains a moving inscription written by Sports Journalist Jeff Powell who was a close friend, biographer and the best man at Moore's marriage to Stephanie.

" Immaculate footballer, Imperial defender, Immortal hero of 1966, First Englishman to raise the World Cup aloft, National treasure, Master of Wembley, Lord of the game, Captain extraordinary, Gentleman for all time.

An impressive sight the statue stands 20 feet tall including the plinth. The statue was commissoned Wembley New Stadium Ltd.

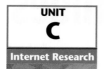

Browsing Subject Guides

Subject guides group information by subject or topic. To find information, you browse the topics, which are usually arranged alphabetically and hierarchically. Many subject guides also allow keyword searching. Subject guides are especially helpful when you have limited knowledge of a topic you need to research. They often allow you to see the breadth of a subject and how it relates to other subjects. Subject guides also focus your search toward more reliable or expert resources. Although subject guides are usually compiled by experts, rather than programs like search engine spiders, you still need to know how to evaluate your results. The Portland City Planning team, overwhelmed with the number of Web sites on alternative energy, wants you to find sites you judge to be especially reliable. Bob Johnson, your friend the reference librarian, suggests using subject guides for this phase of the research process.

OBJECTIVES

Understand subject guides

Browse a subject guide

Search a subject guide

Navigate a subject guide

Tap trailblazer pages

Use a specialized search engine

Understand evaluative criteria

Evaluate a Web page

Understanding Subject Guides

Subject guides emphasize quality over quantity. Unlike search engines, subject guides are usually hand compiled and maintained by experts, offering users greater selectivity and quality of information, but less coverage than search engines. These experts usually annotate the links to resources with useful information. Carefully designed selection criteria are used to select resources to include in subject guides, which are also known as **subject directories**, **Internet directories**, or **subject trees**. Subject guides organize the sites they index into alphabetical and hierarchical topics that you click your way through, to find relevant links. Links are arranged by subject, like books in a library, for easy access. The content of individual subject guides varies from general links to mostly commercial ones to mostly reference or academic links. Some subject guides are maintained in one location by individuals or organizations. **Distributed subject guides** are maintained on computers all over the world. Table C-1 provides more information about several subject guides. You want to become more efficient at searching the Web for reliable information on alternative energy. You decide to follow Bob's suggestion to learn more about subject guides.

DETAILS

Some notable characteristics of subject guides are as follows:

- **Organization**

    Subject guides organize links to Web sites into topical hierarchies. A **hierarchy** is a ranked order. The ranked order typically goes from more general to more specific. For example, the general topics (in **bold**) in the Librarians' Internet Index (LII) subject guide, shown in Figure C-1, are followed by related, more specific topics. Clicking a topic, such as "Science," links to a list of subtopics. Subtopics link to increasingly detailed topics. You navigate or browse a subject guide primarily by "**drilling down**," or clicking through topics and subtopics arranged hierarchically, in increasingly specific subject headings.

QUICK TIP

Differences between subject guides and search engines are disappearing as better guides provide search engines and better engines provide subject categories. Nevertheless, most guides' engines still search only their hand-selected indexes, and most engines' subject categories are still compiled electronically from all sites crawled by their spiders.

- **Selectivity and small size**

    Subject guides are selective. In better subject guides, qualified people rather than computer programs decide which Web pages are worthy of inclusion. Subject guides can provide links to useful sites that search engine spiders are unable to access. They often include **trailblazer pages** or Web pages with links to other sites covering all aspects of a topic. Subject experts also include sites that might cover one or two very detailed subtopics. This kind of selectivity ensures that returned Web pages are some of the best on the subject. Because of this selectivity, subject guides are relatively small, which can be an advantage, saving you the time and trouble of sifting through thousands of search engine results.

- **Access methods**

    In addition to hierarchical lists of topics, better subject guides provide search forms with which you can use keywords to search their indexes. A local search engine allows you to search the titles and the annotations of indexed Web pages. A subject guide might also provide lists of topics arranged in various ways, including alphabetically, geographically, chronologically, or by the Dewey Decimal subject classification system.

QUICK TIP

These annotations are great time-savers, as they provide expert previews of sites for you.

- **Annotations**

    Annotations are summaries or reviews of the contents of a Web page, written by the subject guide contributors, usually experts in the field, such as professionals or academics, or experts in information and the Web, such as librarians. Annotations make subject guides the tools of choice for many researchers.

- **Results**

    Subject guides return fewer results than search engines, but all of the results are more likely to be reliable and useful. Typical subject guide results include the number of results, annotations, and subject terms under which related sites are indexed. The latter can be especially useful when you are just learning about your topic and how it relates to other subjects. Figure C-2 shows one search result out of 24 sites LII returned for the search "renewable energy."

FIGURE C-1: Librarians' Internet Index (LII) home page

Search text box

Alphabetically and hierarchically arranged subject categories and subcategories

Subject categories

Subject subcategories

Link to Help information

Explanation of sponsored results usage

Special features

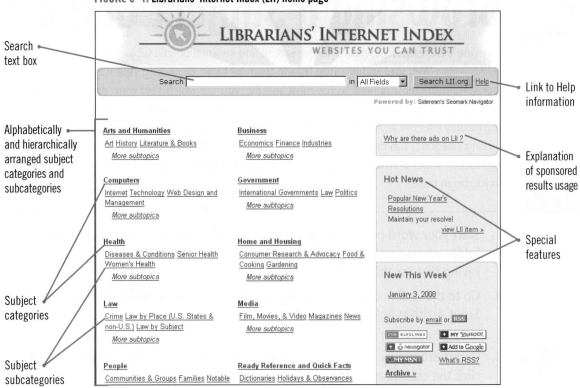

FIGURE C-2: LII sample search result

Option to see related Library of Congress subject headings and more information on the record

Sample annotated search result for "renewable energy"

Options for grouping results

Options for sorting results

Options to comment on or to email the record

Links to the result

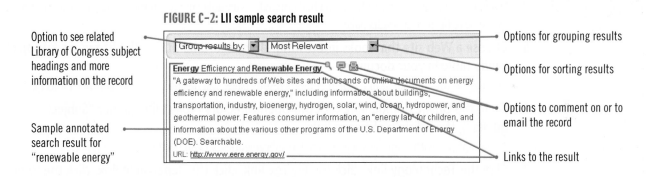

TABLE C-1: Sampling of subject guides (see links to these and more subject guides on the Online Companion at www.course.com/illustrated/research4)

subject guides	type	features
BUBL LINK	Academic/scholarly	Searchable, Dewey #s, UK slant
EERE	Government energy specific	Searchable
INFOMINE	Academic/scholarly/distributed	Searchable, librarians, high quality
Librarians' Internet Index	General/reference	Searchable, librarians, high quality
ipl (The Internet Public Library)	General/reference	Searchable, librarians, university based, high quality
Open Directory Project	General/distributed	Most search engines use, uneven
Scout Archives	Academic/reference	Searchable, university based, high quality
WWW Virtual Library	Academic/general/distributed	First Web subject guide, indexed by subject experts

Browsing a Subject Guide

Browsing is the easiest and most effective way to find information in a subject guide. The creators of subject guides review Web sites and organize links to them by topic. By clicking your way through the hierarchy of topics, from the most general to the most specific, you see which sites were deemed best by the guide's contributors. If you are unsure of keywords when starting your research, browsing a subject guide can help you identify effective keywords. In a distributed subject guide, which is created by a variety of contributors, clicking categories can direct your browser to other sites. You decide to continue your search for information about alternative energy by browsing a few subject guides. Bob recommends the Scout Archives, so you begin there.

STEPS

1. **Start your word-processing program, open the file IR C-1.doc from the drive and folder where you store your Data Files, then save it as Subject Guides where you are saving files for this book**

2. **Go to the Online Companion at www.course.com/illustrated/research4, then click the Scout Archives link (under "Subject guides")**
   You see that you have options for a keyword search, an advanced search, or browsing through subject headings.

QUICK TIP
A subject guide's list of topics offers numerous choices. If the path you drill down doesn't work, navigate back and try another path.

3. **Under Browse by Library of Congress Subject Headings, click on the letter R, then click the classification Renewable energy sources**
   Your results appear and above the list of indexed pages are several classifications or subcategories to further focus your results.

4. **Click on United States**
   Figure C-3 illustrates your results. If you had entered "renewable energy" in the home page search form, this would have been your results page.

5. **Choose a Web site that looks interesting, then record its title in the Browsing a Subject Guide table in your document**
   This page is the equivalent of a search engine's results page. You decide to explore another subject guide.

6. **Go to the Online Companion, click the Open Directory Project link (under "Subject guides"), then click the Science link**
   A page appears with numerous science-related subcategories, so you need to make a choice.

7. **Click the Technology link, click the Energy link, click the Renewable link, click the Wind link, then click the Windmills link**
   You have drilled down through over 100,000 results for Science to very few for Windmills, going from the more general to the more specific. Your end results page should look similar to Figure C-4.

8. **Choose a title that looks interesting, record it in the same table, then save your document**

FIGURE C-3: Scout Archives drill-down results

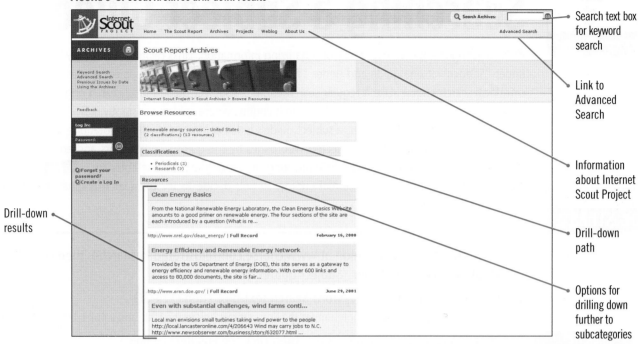

Search text box for keyword search

Link to Advanced Search

Information about Internet Scout Project

Drill-down path

Options for drilling down further to subcategories

Drill-down results

FIGURE C-4: Open Directory drill-down results

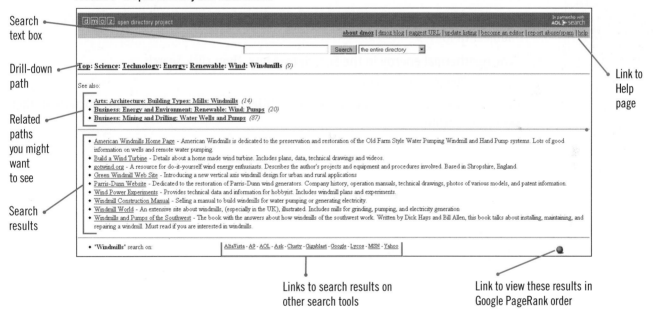

Search text box

Drill-down path

Related paths you might want to see

Search results

Link to Help page

Links to search results on other search tools

Link to view these results in Google PageRank order

Understanding distributed subject guides

WWW Virtual Library and the Open Directory Project are examples of distributed subject guides. **Distributed subject guides** are created by a variety of contributors working somewhat independently. Each group or person is usually responsible for a subtopic of a main topic. These guides are said to be "distributed" because rather than being on one computer, the Web pages for different parts of the guide are stored on different computers, distributed around the country or around the world. Because distributed subject guides have many contributors working independently, each with varying levels of expertise and resources, distributed subject guides tend to have an uneven quality and a lack of standardization. However, this potential downside is balanced by the fact that these different parts of the guide's index are usually maintained by subject experts with a high level of awareness of what is available on the Web in their field.

Searching a Subject Guide

Each subject guide has a unique way of organizing information. Links relating to "Energy" might appear under "Science" at one guide and under "Technology" at another. Most subject guides also offer their own local search engine. Like a regular search engine, a subject guide's local search engine searches its own indexes to return results. But unlike a search engine, whose spiders constantly crawl the Web adding the full text of pages to its indexes, a subject guide's index contains only the annotations, keywords, and subject headings assigned to the selected Web pages by the guide's contributors and editors, who are often either experts in the field they are indexing or research experts like librarians. You need more reliable Web sites on geothermal energy, so you decide to try the search engines in the Scout Archives and Open Directory.

STEPS

1. **Go to the Online Companion at www.course.com/illustrated/research4, then click the Scout Archives link (under "Subject guides")**

2. **Type geothermal in the Keyword Search text box, then click GO**
   Scout Archives provides an annotation for the link, a direct link to the URL, and a link labeled Full Record.

QUICK TIP

Remember that Web sites redesign their pages frequently. If you don't see an element mentioned in the steps, look around the page for a similarly labeled element.

3. **Choose a record from your results, then click the Full Record link**
   Your results should look similar to Figure C-5.

4. **Record the title of the record you chose in the Searching a Subject Guide table in your document**

5. **Go to the Online Companion, then click the Open Directory Project link (under "Subject guides")**

6. **Type geothermal energy in the Search text box, then click Search**
   Figure C-6 illustrates your results.

7. **Choose a site that interests you, record its title in the same table in your document, then save your document**

FIGURE C-5: Scout Archives Full Record of a search result

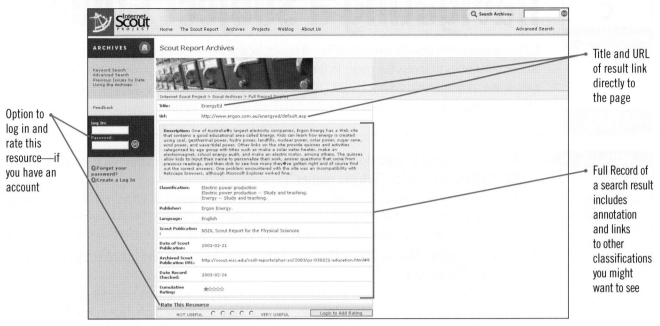

Title and URL of result link directly to the page

Option to log in and rate this resource—if you have an account

Full Record of a search result includes annotation and links to other classifications you might want to see

FIGURE C-6: Open Directory Search results

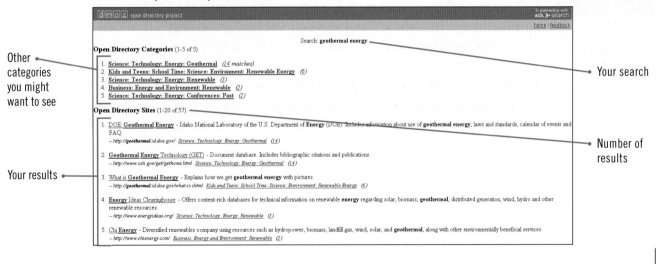

Other categories you might want to see

Your search

Number of results

Your results

Navigating a Subject Guide

Subject guides might provide hierarchical lists of topics, local search engines, geographical lists, alphabetical lists, or other ways to access the pages in their databases. BUBL LINK also indexes by the Dewey Decimal system, the same numeric subject classification system used in many libraries. Bob mentions this interesting feature in BUBL (pronounced *bubble*) and you decide to try it.

STEPS

1. **Go to the Online Companion at www.course.com/illustrated/research4, then click the BUBL LINK link (under "Subject guides")**

   The BUBL home page opens, as shown in Figure C-7. You can navigate this subject guide in several ways, including by Dewey Decimal classifications, A to Z links, alphabetical Subject Menus, Countries, and Types of resources. BUBL also provides basic and advanced searching. You decide to explore a few of these options.

2. **Click the Subject Menus link at the top of the page, look over the list of subjects, then click the Energy link**

   The alphabetical list of topics under "Subject Menus" is a way to start browsing or drilling down through subjects from a more comprehensive list than the broad headings on the home page. The subtopics under "Energy" include their corresponding Dewey Decimal numbers. You decide to click a Dewey number.

3. **Click the 333.79 Renewable energy link**

   BUBL provides useful information, including site authors. Now you decide to try the alphabetical index.

4. **On the A-Z links at the top of the page, click the R link, then click the renewable energy link**

   Figure C-8 illustrates your results. BUBL displays the results in two ways: On the left side for easy previewing, BUBL lists the titles, as links, of the Web pages indexed under the term "Renewable energy." To the right, BUBL lists the titles, as well as their annotations and other information, such as Dewey Classification, Resource type, Author, and other subject headings for this title. Now you want to try searching by Dewey number.

5. **Near the top of the page, click the Home link**

6. **Click the 300 Social sciences link, on the next page click the 330 Economics link, then click the 333 Environment and economics of land and energy link**

   This page should look familiar. You reached the same page in Step 2 when you navigated the guide using the Subject menus.

7. **Click the 333.79 Renewable energy link, choose one site, record its title in the Navigating a Subject Guide table in your document, then save your document**

   This page should also look familiar. This is the same list you found in Step 3; you just reached it through a different route.

FIGURE C-7: BUBL home page

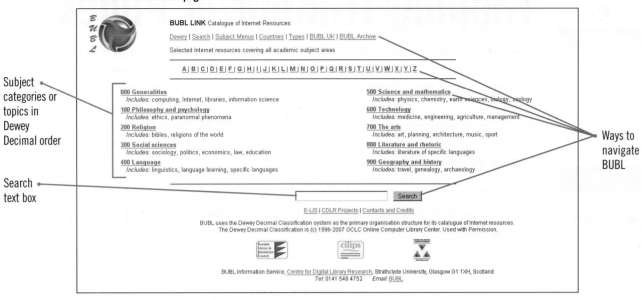

Subject categories or topics in Dewey Decimal order

Search text box

Ways to navigate BUBL

FIGURE C-8: BUBL A to Z results

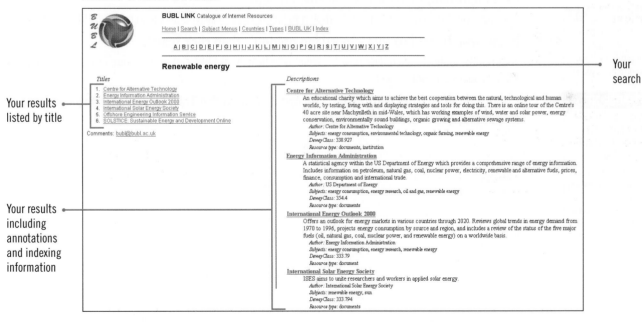

Your results listed by title

Your results including annotations and indexing information

Your search

Tapping Trailblazer Pages

Trailblazer pages are resources that organize and provide links to recommended Web sites in a specific field or subject area. The best ones are created by scholars, experts, and organizations. Trailblazer pages are an excellent source of reliable Web resources. These pages can be narrow or broad in scope, but all attempt to provide thorough coverage of their subjects. They usually provide not only links to useful sites, but also several logical, well-organized ways of navigating them. ▓▓▓▓ You want to familiarize yourself with trailblazer pages. You decide to explore a site Bob recommends—the U.S. Department of Energy's Energy Efficiency and Renewable Energy (EERE) site.

STEPS

TROUBLE
Many Web sites change appearance often. Usually the information remains the same; however, you might need to locate and click slightly different links to find it.

1. **Go to the Online Companion at www.course.com/illustrated/research4, then click the EERE link (under "Subject guides")**
   EERE provides several ways to navigate the site.

2. **Click the Subject Index link**
   The Subject Index page opens, as shown in Figure C-9. Browsing the subject areas covered by EERE gives you an idea of its coverage.

3. **Click your browser's Back button to return to the home page, then click the Site Name Index link and explore this page**
   Browsing the Web sites that EERE indexes by name gives you an idea of its quality.

4. **Click your browser's Back button to return to the home page, then explore the home page, looking for other ways to navigate the site**

5. **Click the Solar Energy Technologies link under "Programs," click Photovoltaics, click Why PV is Important, then click To the Environment**
   The page you drilled down to opens, as shown in Figure C-10. Now you decide to try the EERE search engine.

TROUBLE
If your search produces no results, try it again but without the quotation marks.

6. **In the Search text box, type "portland oregon", then click Search**
   Your results, as illustrated in Figure C-11, seem to indicate that EERE can provide numerous links to reliable Web resources for your project.

QUICK TIP
Whenever you find a great site, such as EERE, that you know you will want to reference again, save it in your Bookmarks, Favorites, or on your Links bar so you can get back to it easily.

7. **Choose one site from your results, record its title in the Trailblazer Pages table in your document, then save your document**

Finding Trailblazer Pages

Library Web pages that list online resources for a subject area are good trailblazer pages. Librarians often create trailblazer pages for specific classes or subject areas, so ask for suggestions at your library's reference desk. You can also ask an instructor in the field for suggestions. If you know the name of an expert, look for links on their Web page. Whenever you find a good site in a subject area, check out its Links page, which serves as a trailblazer page. Subject guides are one of the best places to find trailblazer pages. Smaller, specialized subject guides serve as trailblazer pages themselves by providing links to recommended sites in a subject area. The WWW Virtual Library is an excellent trailblazer resource. The Online Companion provides a link to it under "Subject guides."

FIGURE C-9: EERE home page

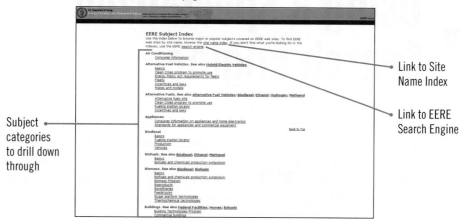

Subject
categories
to drill down
through

Link to Site
Name Index

Link to EERE
Search Engine

FIGURE C-10: EERE drill-down results

Other sub-
headings
under "Solar
Energy
Technologies"

The page you
drilled down
to under
"Photovoltaics"

FIGURE C-11: EERE search results

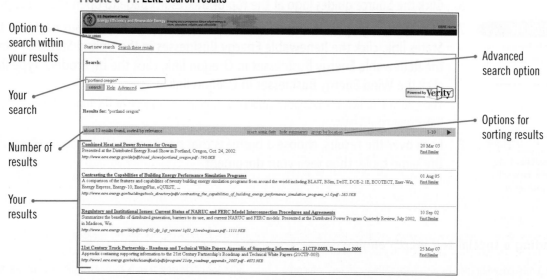

Option to
search within
your results

Your
search

Number of
results

Your
results

Advanced
search option

Options for
sorting results

Using a Specialized Search Engine

Search engines often find too many results and subject guides might provide fewer than you need. Specialized search engines can combine the best features of both. **Specialized search engines** act similarly to regular Web search engines, except, like some subject guides, they limit the Web pages they search by subject. Specialized search engines are available for a wide variety of topics, including law, medicine, computers, and energy. ▓▓▓▓▓ Bob mentions that the specialized search engine, Source for Renewable Energy, is a good place to locate alternative energy resources on the Web. You decide to use it to see if you can find out who sells wind energy equipment in Portland.

STEPS

1. **Go to the Online Companion at www.course.com/illustrated/research4, then click The Source for Renewable Energy link (under "Specialized search engines")**

   Figure C-12 illustrates the site's home page. As in other subject guides, there are multiple ways to search, but you want to explore the specialized search engine.

2. **Click the Search the Business Guide link to open the site's specialized search engine**

   QUICK TIP

   Remember that you can but don't need to capitalize proper nouns/names for search tools.

3. **In the Search text box, type "wind energy" "portland oregon", make sure both of your phrases are in quotation marks and that the SourceGuides.com button is selected, then click Search**

   When both keyword phrases are in quotation marks, the search engine interprets your search correctly. Figure C-13 illustrates your search results page. It should look familiar—Google provides the search technology for this site.

4. **Scroll through the results, noting that each link's URL begins with "energy.sourceguides"**

5. **Click a link that looks interesting, noting the products or services offered and contact information, then record the name in the Using a Specialized Search Engine table in your document**

   The fact that each link's URL begins with the same domain indicates that you only searched this specialized site, not the Web. Now you decide to try accessing this information another way.

6. **Click the Source guides logo at the top of the results page to open the home page**

   QUICK TIP

   You might have to scroll down to find the links.

7. **Click the geographic location link, click the Renewable Energy Businesses in the United States link, click the Renewable Energy Businesses in the United States by State link, click the Renewable Energy Businesses in Oregon link, click the by Product Type link, then click the Wind Energy Businesses in Oregon link**

   The path you drilled down appears under the Source Guides logo at the top of the page. Figure C-14 illustrates your results page.

   TROUBLE

   If no result has a site, record the name of one of your results.

8. **Look over the results, choose a business that has its own Web page, record the URL in the same table, then save your document**

Finding a specialized search engine

Ask a reference librarian or instructor if they can recommend a specialized search engine for your research topic. Sometimes library Web pages that list resources in a subject area provide links to specialized search engines. Trailblazer pages and subject guides can also provide links. See the Online Companion for links to several specialized search engines.

FIGURE C-12: The Source for Renewable Energy home page

Ways to navigate the site

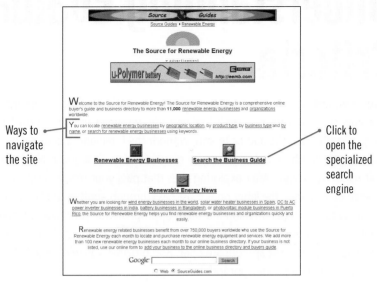

Click to open the specialized search engine

FIGURE C-13: The Source for Renewable Energy phrase search results

Your search

Source Guides logo

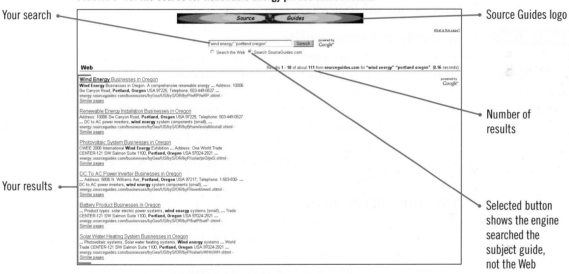

Number of results

Your results

Selected button shows the engine searched the subject guide, not the Web

FIGURE C-14: The Source for Renewable Energy drill-down results

Drill-down path

Related results

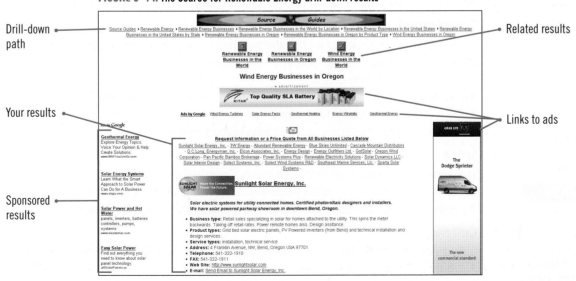

Your results

Links to ads

Sponsored results

Understanding Evaluative Criteria

Evaluative criteria are standards used to determine if a Web site is appropriate for your needs. No matter what your subject or which search tool you use, resources you find must be evaluated. Web information can go directly from the author to you, without the intervening editorial or review process used for most printed material. This requires you to be discriminating. First you evaluate search results to choose which result pages to explore. After exploring sites that pass your search results evaluation, you eliminate some and keep others. Then the latter ones must pass through another level of assessment. Figure C-15 illustrates the criteria to use in determining if a site is appropriate for your needs. Figure C-16 shows an example of identifying evaluative criteria on a Web page. You found so many sites that you are concerned about selecting the most appropriate ones. Bob provides you with criteria to use to evaluate Web pages to determine which pages are appropriate.

DETAILS

Criteria include the following:

QUICK TIP

If there is an email link for the author or owner, you can write and ask questions about your research.

- **Authority and accountability**
  Knowing the author's or owner's identity is key to determining how reliable the site is. This is usually the most important criterion to apply. Consider these questions:
  - Is the author or owner clearly identified? Are qualifications and associations identified?
  - Is there contact information for the author or owner? Is there About information?
  - Is there an association with a university, a government agency, or an organization? If so, are there links?
  - Has the author written in the field? Does the owner specialize in the field?
  - What kind of results do you get from a search on the author or owner?
  - Is there a bibliography? Are resources well documented?

- **Objectivity and accuracy**
  A site's objectivity and accuracy greatly affect its appropriateness. Nothing is wrong with selling a product or advocating an idea, but that should be stated as the site's purpose. Consider these questions:
  - Does the author state the purpose of the site? Is the content presented as fact or as opinion?
  - Is the publisher, sponsor, or host for the site identified?
  - What do other Web sites or articles say about the author or sponsor?
  - Is the site indexed in a subject guide or trailblazer page? If so, is the URL the same?

- **Organization**
  The way a Web site is organized is often almost as important as its content. Great content on a page can be defeated by poor design and functionality. Attractiveness and graphic features can mask a lack of meaningful content. Consider these questions:
  - Is the site well designed and functional? Is there a site map and Help page?
  - Is it easy to navigate? Do navigational buttons and internal links work?
  - Is it searchable? Are there a variety of ways to access material?

- **Scope**
  The **scope** of a site is the range of topics it covers. Consider these questions:
  - Is there introductory or summary information describing the scope of the site?
  - Who is the intended audience? Is it useful for professionals? Laypeople? Students?

QUICK TIP

Check the site's home page or About page to look for dates, or try the site map to find the most logical page to check.

- **Currency**
  Currency or timeliness might or might not be an issue for your search. Consider these questions:
  - Is there a creation or revision date?
  - Are there many broken links? If so, this might indicate the site is not being maintained.

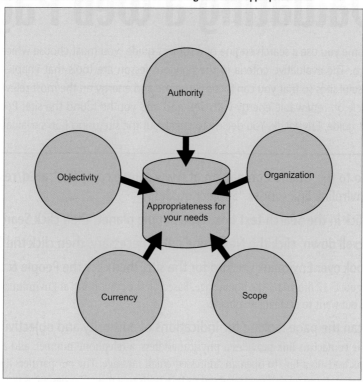

FIGURE C-16: Identifying evaluative criteria on the DSIRE home page

Page name describes site and indicates **scope**

Scope indicated in page summary

Link to more information about what the site provides and how to use it indicate **organization**

Useful external links serve as trailblazer page

Easy navigation to pages, links, and resources indicate **organization**

Currency indicated by date the site was last updated

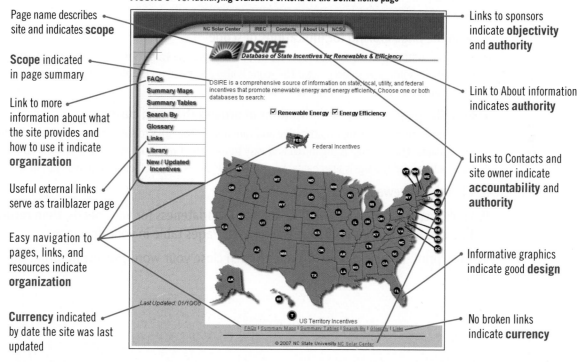

Links to sponsors indicate **objectivity** and **authority**

Link to About information indicates **authority**

Links to Contacts and site owner indicate **accountability** and **authority**

Informative graphics indicate good **design**

No broken links indicate **currency**

Evaluating Web page objectivity

No Web page is totally objective. Commercial sites (.com) usually exist to sell something. Nonprofit organizations (.org) have opinions about their causes. Even an educational page (.edu) can be affected by its creator's views. Ideally, these sites divulge their positions openly, but very often you have to dig around to find out. Educational (.edu) and government (.gov) sites generally are more objective, or at least support their ideas with documented facts. As long as you can ascertain a page's bias, you can come to your own conclusions about its content.

Evaluating a Web Page

Every time you use a search engine or a subject guide, you must choose which Web sites to include in your research. The evaluative criteria in the previous lesson are tools that enable you to quickly eliminate the least useful sites so that you can focus your time and energy on the most relevant ones. ▰▰▰ Bob shares an article on renewable energy with you and tells you he found the site, People & the Planet, through a subject guide, Envirolink. You decide to check out the site using Bob's evaluative criteria.

STEPS

TROUBLE

Remember that sites often change their appearance. But if a site has moved or disappeared from the Web, the Online Companion will link to a new site and provide new directions to follow.

1. **Go to the Online Companion at www.course.com/illustrated/research4, then click the Envirolink link (under "Subject guides")**

2. **Click in the Search text box, type people planet, then click Search**

3. **Scroll down, click the Next Page link if necessary, then click the People & the Planet link**

4. **Look over Envirolink's record for the site, then click the People & the Planet title or URL link**

   Figure C-17 illustrates the home page. Based on the description at Envirolink, you already feel positive about it, but want to evaluate it yourself.

5. **Scan the page looking for indications of authority and objectivity**

   The contact us link provides a physical address, a telephone number, and an email address. The feedback link leads to a link to open an addressed email message. The our partners link leads to a page that links to numerous organizations. The about us link leads to a page that describes the scope of the site, lists names of those involved with the site, and lists the members of an international advisory board, including names and organizations. It also lists and links to the site's sponsors. You decide the authority, accountability, and objectivity of this site seem excellent.

6. **Scan the page looking for indications of scope**

   There is a summary of the site's purpose on the home page. The scope is indicated from the home page links to internal resources by subject areas. The scope is also addressed on the about us page. You decide you have a good understanding of the scope of the site.

7. **Scan the page looking for indications of organization and currency**

   You already think the design is attractive and functional. The links to subject areas and latest online show recent dates. The site map is organized and easy to use. All of the links work, there are several ways to find information, and the site is searchable. You decide this site is very well organized and current.

8. **Click the Renewable Energy link**

9. **Look over the page, consider the site's appropriateness for your needs, then record the title and date posted in the Evaluating Web Pages table in your document**

10. **Save, print, and close your document, then close your word-processing program**

FIGURE C-17: People & the Planet home page

Information about owners, sponsors, partners, and individuals associated with the site

Summary shows site's purpose

Easy navigation to internal resources by subject areas

Feedback link

Different ways to navigate site

Top of home page

Last update current

Latest online postings current

Appropriate graphics

Author name provided

Site map

Contact information

Bottom of home page

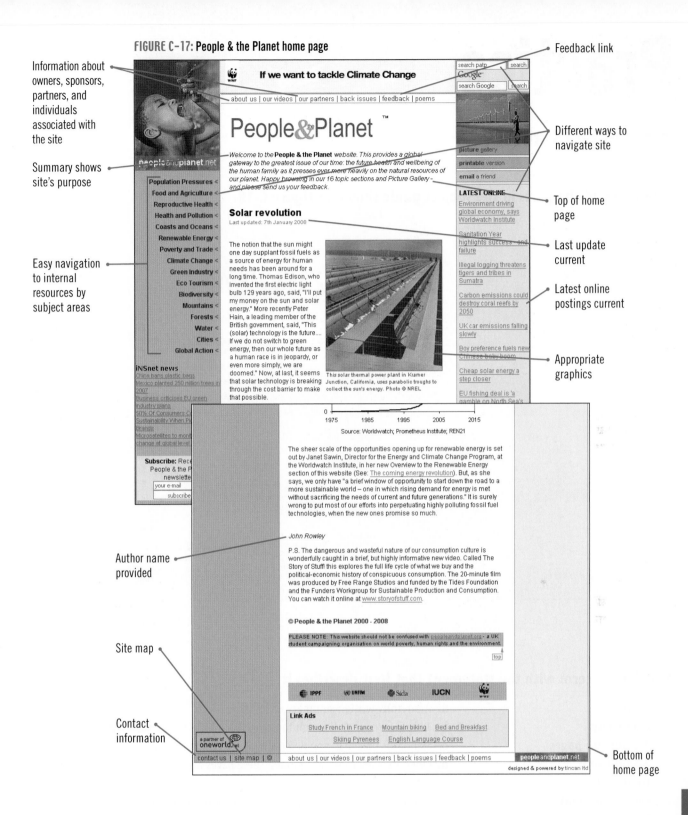

Practice

▼ CONCEPTS REVIEW

Label each of the parts in the subject guide shown in Figure C-18.

FIGURE C-18

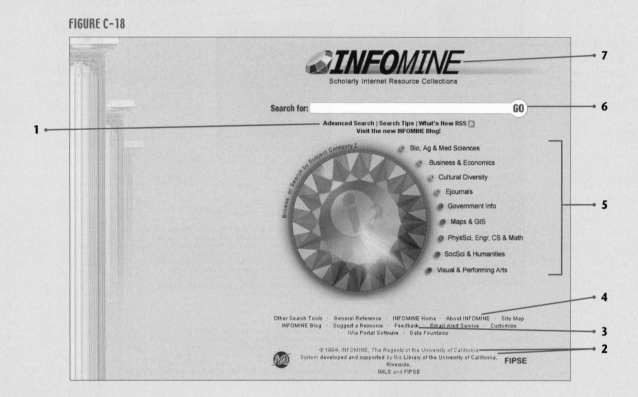

Match each term with the statement that best describes it.

8. Scope
9. Hierarchy
10. Trailblazer pages
11. Annotation
12. Drill down
13. Dewey Decimal
14. Subject guide
15. Specialized search engine
16. Evaluative criteria
17. Distributed

a. A carefully written summary or review

b. To browse or click through topics to reach links on a results page

c. Standards that help you determine if a Web site is right for your needs

d. Often indexed in subject guides, these pages link to valuable sites, usually subject specific

e. A subject guide compiled by numerous editors and stored on numerous computers

f. Combines some of the best features of both a subject guide and a search engine

g. A ranked order

h. A subject classification system used by many libraries and some subject guides

i. A search tool, usually created by subject experts, that organizes annotated links by topics and subtopics

j. The range of topics a site covers; it can be broad or narrow

Select the best answer from the list of choices.

18. **Traits that all subject guides share:**
    a. Are organized hierarchically and are selective in the Web sites they list
    b. Are relatively small compared with search engines
    c. Include annotations to the Web sites
    d. All of the above

19. **One definition of browsing is:**
    a. Clicking through the hierarchy of topics at a subject guide.
    b. Using a local search engine to search a subject guide.
    c. Using criteria to evaluate a Web site.
    d. Finding out who wrote a Web page.

20. **A distributed subject guide:**
    a. Is maintained by one editor.
    b. Usually resides on one computer.
    c. Is the same thing as a search engine.
    d. Might lack standardization.

21. **An annotated subject guide:**
    a. Allows you to write reviews of Web sites.
    b. Contains summaries of Web sites.
    c. Reviews other subject guides.
    d. Allows you to search for reviews of search engines.

22. **Which is *not* a way subject guides are organized?**
    a. Alphabetically
    b. By hexadecimal
    c. By Dewey Decimal
    d. Topically

23. **Specialized search engines:**
    a. Only exist on a few topics.
    b. Are like a regular search engine except they index far more Web pages.
    c. Cannot be queried using Boolean operators.
    d. Share qualities of both subject guides and search engines.

24. **Which is a common way to find a specialized search engine?**
    a. Ask a librarian or professor.
    b. See if there is a link to one from a trailblazer page or a subject guide.
    c. Look for a link to one from a library Web page listing resources in a subject area.
    d. All of the above

25. **When evaluating a Web page to determine its authority, you should *not*:**
    a. Consider the qualifications of the author or owner of a Web page.
    b. Consider the conviction with which an author writes.
    c. Look to see what else the author has written.
    d. Look to see if the page is associated with a university.

▼ SKILLS REVIEW

1. Understand subject guides.

  a. Open the file IR C-2.doc from the drive and folder where you store your Data Files, save it as **Using Subject Guides** where you are saving files for this book, then add your name at the top of the document.

  b. Choose at least three of the five common traits of subject guides mentioned in the Understanding Subject Guides lesson.

  c. In the Skill #1 table in your document, write a few sentences about how these traits make subject guides useful for Web research and different from search engines.

  d. Save your document.

2. Browse a subject guide.

  a. A friend is interested in changing careers and asks you to help her find information on companies offering good opportunities for a working mother.

  b. Start your browser and go to the Online Companion at www.course.com/illustrated/research4.

  c. Click the Librarians' Internet Index link (under "Subject guides").

  d. Look over the general topics and click the Business link.

  e. Look over the subtopics under Business, and then click Jobs & Work.

  f. In the resulting subtopics, click Women.

  g. Look over these annotations, as illustrated in Figure C-19, and choose one that looks appropriate for this search.

  h. In the Skill #2 table in your document, record the title of the Web site you chose, then save your document.

FIGURE C-19

3. Search a subject guide.

  a. You are writing a book and want to avoid plagiarizing the information you read.

  b. Go to the Online Companion, then click the INFOMINE link (under "Subject guides").

  c. In the Search for text box, type **plagiarism**, then click GO.

  d. In the Skill #3 table in your document, record how many Web sites are listed.

  e. Follow one link, choose a site, record the title in the same table, then save your document.

4. Navigate a subject guide.

  a. Your younger brother is writing a report for his high school Social Studies class about families in Canada. He has one statistics book with some good information in it, but would like more. You notice the book has the Dewey number 310 on it. You decide to look in BUBL using the Dewey number for more information.

  b. Go to the Online Companion, then click link to BUBL LINK (under "Subject guides").

  c. Click 300 Social sciences.

  d. On the next page, click 310 Collections of general statistics.

  e. On the next page, click 317.3 Statistics of the United States and Canada.

  f. In the Skill #4 table in your document, record the total number of Web sites listed under this link.

  g. Look through the links and their annotations. Choose one that you think might be useful for your brother. Record its title, then save your document.

5. Tap trailblazer pages.

  a. You are still keeping your eye open for online career material for your friend and have just run across The Occupational Outlook Handbook. You want to decide quickly if this is one that you want to share with her.

  b. Go to the Online Companion, then click the Occupational Outlook Handbook link under "Specialized search engines."

  c. Answer the questions posed in the Skill #5 table in your document, then save your document.

▼ SKILLS REVIEW (CONTINUED)

6. Use a specialized search engine.

a. You remember reading a great hockey-related quote, but can't quite recall how it was worded. It might have been by Wayne Gretzky and it had something to do with the phrase "100% of your shots." You decide to try a specialty subject engine to find it.

b. Go to the Online Companion, then click the Quoteland.com link under "Specialized search engines."

c. Click in the Search text box, type the keywords you remember from the quote: **100% shots**, then click Search.

d. Look at the quotes on the results page and identify the one you are looking for.

e. Record the quote in the Skill #6 table in your document, then save your document.

7. Understand evaluative criteria.

a. In the Skill #7 table in your document, identify at least three criteria for evaluating Web pages for appropriateness.

b. In the same table, write a few sentences about each of the three criteria, including why the criteria are important and sample questions to answer to determine if the page meets the criteria.

c. Save your document.

8. Evaluate a Web page.

a. You are writing a paper on the history of mathematics. You found a Web page that might be relevant and want to evaluate it quickly.

b. Go to the Online Companion, then click the MacTutor History of Mathematics link under "Specialized search engines."

c. Answer the questions in the Skill #8 table in your document, then print, save, and close your document.

▼ INDEPENDENT CHALLENGE 1

Your company is thinking of designing new billboards and the graphic artist, who wants to use a retro look in one of her proposals, asks you to help her find examples of World War II poster art. You want to find something for her that you're sure is of good quality, so you turn to the INFOMINE subject guide.

a. Open the Online Companion at www.course.com/illustrated/research4, then click INFOMINE.

b. There are a couple of potential broad headings on the home page that might produce good results. Click the Government Info link.

c. When the search page opens, scroll if necessary to Browse Options for Government Information, then click Subjects.

d. In the list of the alphabet, click the W link, then click the appropriate letter range link to find World War.

e. Scroll down the alphabetical list until you find World War, 1939 – 1945 – Posters, then click the heading.

FIGURE C-20

f. Start a new document in your word processor, add your name, then save it as **WWII Posters** where you are saving files for this book.

g. Record several indexed titles, print the document, then save it.

Advanced Challenge Exercise

■ Click the link for World War II Poster Database.

■ Look over the site, as shown in Figure C-20, and identify ways to navigate it.

■ Start a new document and save it as **WWII Posters ACE**.

■ Write a few sentences about how you can navigate this site.

■ Perform a search and identify a poster you find interesting, then display the full record to find out more about it.

■ In your document, describe your search, and provide information about the poster you selected.

h. Add your name to your document, save it, print it, then close your document.

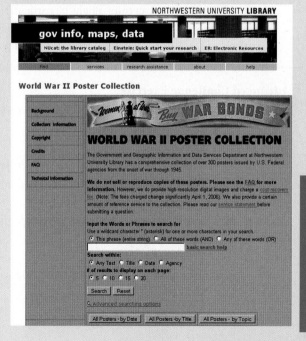

Internet Research

▼ INDEPENDENT CHALLENGE 2

The healthcare provider you work for has just posted a new Web page. The managers found the Web site shown in Figure C-21 and want you to evaluate it for them. Is it credible and good enough to include as a link on their Web page? They want you to present a list of reasons why it should or should not be included.

a. Find this page on the Web.

b. Evaluate the Web site by considering its organization, authority, scope, objectivity, and currency.

c. In your word processor, start a new document and save it as **Web site evaluation** where you are saving files for this book.

d. List your thoughts on why this site would or would not be an appropriate link on your employer's site.

FIGURE C-21

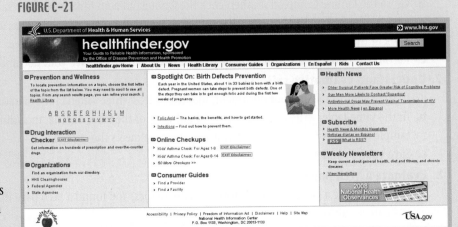

e. Include at least five reasons in your argument, basing them on evaluative criteria.

f. Add your name to the document, then save, print, and close it.

▼ INDEPENDENT CHALLENGE 3

You have a class assignment due for which you must use a credible Web site as one of your sources for a paper covering a topic of your choosing. You want to use a subject guide of academic quality to locate an appropriate site.

a. Go to a subject guide of your choice.

b. Find a few sources that you think might be useful for your chosen topic.

c. In your word processor, start a new document and save it as **My subject guide** where you are saving files for this book.

d. Describe which subject guide you used and how you searched (local search engine, drilling down, or another method).

e. How many sites did you find related to your topic?

f. Select one site that you think might be particularly relevant and evaluate it according to these criteria: organization, authority, scope, objectivity, and currency. Write at least one sentence about how the site meets each criterion.

g. Would you say this is an appropriate and credible Web site for your assignment?

h. Add your name to the document, save it, and print it.

Advanced Challenge Exercise

- You want to do another search to check for a site you might like better than the one you found in your last search, so you select a different subject guide.
- Find relevant sites.
- Start a new document and save it as **My subject guide ACE**.
- Describe which subject guide you used and how you searched (using a search form or drilling down).
- Record how many sites you found.
- Write a few sentences about which subject guide was the most user friendly and which provided the single best result.

i. Save, print, and close your document, then exit your word-processing program.

▼ REAL LIFE INDEPENDENT CHALLENGE

The first step in getting a job interview in today's highly competitive job market is to create a top-notch résumé. Subject guides can provide invaluable resources to help you prepare the best possible résumé. Because the Open Directory Project is the most comprehensive hand-crafted subject guide on the Web, you decide to check it for help with your résumé.

a. Go to the Online Companion, then click the Open Directory Project link under "Subject guides."

b. Click the Business category, click the Employment category, click Job Search, then click Resume Advice. (Sometimes exact names of categories change, so click the categories that seem most appropriate if what you see is slightly different.)

c. Click one of the resources listed, as shown in Figure C-22, such as Monster. (In addition to résumé advice, Monster is a great place to check for job listings.)

d. Explore the suggestions and examples of how to prepare a résumé.

e. Start a new document called **Resume** and add your name at the top of the page.

f. Record the name and URL of the resource you used.

g. Write a one- or two-paragraph summary of the best tips you find on creating a top-notch résumé.

FIGURE C-22

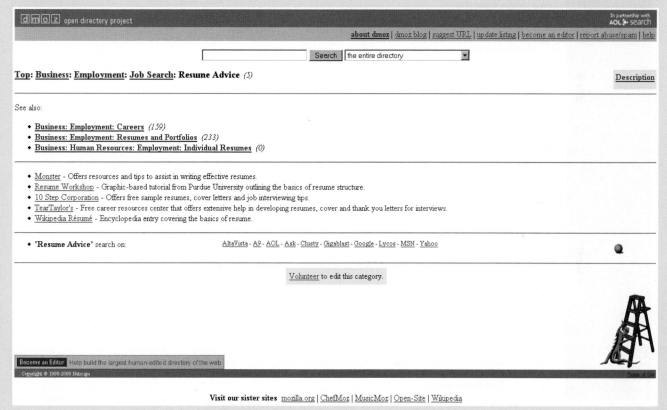

▼ VISUAL WORKSHOP

During your exploration of subject guides, you found and printed the page shown in Figure C-23. Now you want to go back and quickly evaluate it. Go to the Online Companion at www.course.com/illustrated/research4, then click **Google Directory** (under "Subject guides"). Find the site by following this path: **Sports** > **Cricket** > **Statistics** > **HowSTAT**. (*Hint*: Look at site names carefully.) Once at the site, find this page by clicking **Other Cricket Sites** under "Links." Print the page and write your name at the top. Then, start a new document in your word processor, save it as **Cricket Trailblazer Page** where you are saving files for this book, and describe how you think the site meets evaluative criteria. Record your name at the top of the page and attach it to your printout.

FIGURE C-23

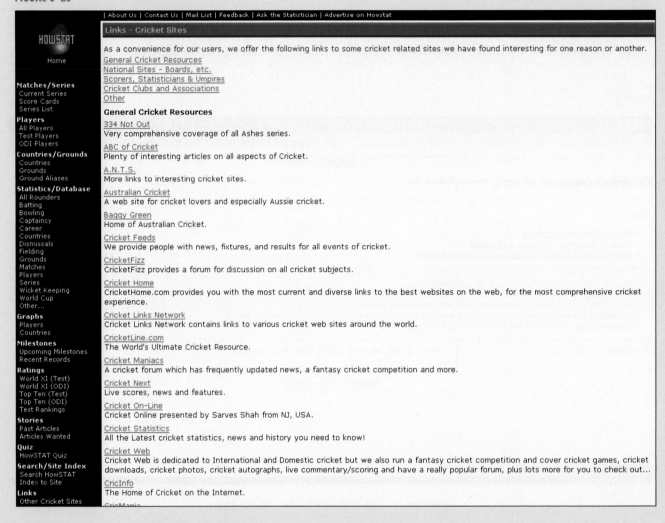

Finding Specialty Information

You have already learned to use search engines and subject guides for general research. However, sometimes the information you want is very specific, such as someone's name, the address of a business, or the definition of a word. This kind of specialty information is often stored in online databases that require direct access, making traditional search engines and most subject guides ineffective. You can find specialty information through specialty Web sites that include online telephone directories, maps, periodicals, government sites, videos, and blogs. Fortunately, specialty search engines and directories make it easier to locate the information stored in many of these Web databases. You will be attending a conference in Washington, D.C., on renewable energy. In preparing for this conference, you speak with Bob Johnson, your friend the reference librarian. He suggests you continue your research on alternative energy using specialty search engines and directories.

OBJECTIVES

Understand specialty information

Find people and places

Locate businesses

Search periodical databases

Find government information

Find online reference sources

Search vertically

Join the social search

Understanding Specialty Information

By far, the largest part of the Internet is hidden from most search tools. This hidden content is called the **deep Web** or the **invisible Web**. The search engines you have used so far search for information on the **surface Web** or **visible Web**, which is the portion of the Web indexed by traditional search engine spiders. Deep Web content largely resides in online databases and is unavailable to traditional search engines and subject guides because these databases require direct queries at their sites. Common examples of databases are online phone books or newspaper and magazine archives. Other examples include **dynamically generated Web pages** that a database creates based on a specific query, or pages that require a login name and password. Figure D-1 provides a conceptual view of Internet content searched by traditional search engines and subject guides contrasted with the content searched by specialty search tools. ▓▓▓▓▓ Not wanting to ignore a large part of the information available via the Internet, you decide to learn about research tools that can help make the invisible Web usable. Bob provides some basics on using these specialty search tools.

DETAILS

The following are important points to remember when using specialty search tools:

* **How to find specialty information**

  Typically, you locate hidden Web content by going to a specialty Web site and using its search form to query a database. Although much of the invisible Web is available publicly, some specialized databases require subscriptions. Because libraries pay the subscription fees for many of these specialty sites, they are a good place to access these resources. For example, many libraries subscribe to specialty search engines and directories, such as the full-text magazine and newspaper article databases ProQuest, EBSCOhost, and InfoTrac. You can also go to a "virtual library" such as The Internet Public Library (www.ipl.org), which links to these specialty Web sites from its reference section.

QUICK TIP

Most specialty search tools have an About or Help link, which explains their focus.

* **Scope and focus**

  By definition, specialty search engines and directories tend to have a narrower and deeper focus, usually resulting in higher-quality content. However, even two tools that focus on the same narrow area are not exactly alike. For example, various governmental agencies are charged with creating access to different, but sometimes overlapping, government information. The National Technical Information Service (NTIS) has a database of publications on scientific, technical, and business-related topics. The U.S. Census Bureau database primarily focuses on Web sites containing demographic information, but also features data related to business, as well as Census Bureau products, such as CD-ROMs and DVDs offered for sale. The Government Printing Office (GPO) is charged with making much of the information produced by the federal government accessible to citizens. State governments also usually provide their own searchable sites.

QUICK TIP

After registering with some "free" sites, you might see an increase in promotional email, either from the site itself or from businesses to which they sold your address. This is the true price you pay for giving the site personal information. Always review the site's privacy information before sharing your address.

* **Free or pay?**

  Most specialty Web sites are either free or partially free. If they are commercial sites, they might give away some information but charge you for detailed data. Other sites might allow you free access, but require you to register with them—some require only an email address or username and others require considerably more personal information. Some sites, including many newspaper sites, allow free access to their most recent files, but charge for access to archival files. If a site is going to charge you up front, it requires your credit card number—so don't give it out unless you want them to use it.

* **Incomplete coverage**

  Up-to-date, detailed information about people or businesses is hard to come by and, therefore, valuable. Companies guard proprietary information with security measures that prevent unauthorized access. So, although specialty Web sites provide access to much of the invisible Web, portions remain hidden.

FIGURE D-1: Internet content searched by traditional search tools contrasted with content searched by specialty search tools*

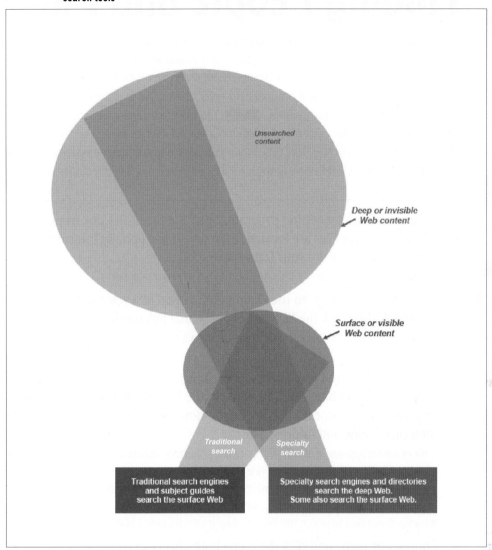

Unsearched content

Deep or invisible Web content

Surface or visible Web content

Traditional search

Specialty search

Traditional search engines and subject guides search the surface Web

Specialty search engines and directories search the deep Web. Some also search the surface Web.

* Conceptual only. If this figure were to scale, the deep Web portion would be dozens of times larger than the surface Web.

Comparing the visible and invisible Web

It is impossible to know the exact size of the invisible or deep Web; however, a conservative estimate places it at approximately 900 billion pages of information, whereas the visible or surface Web contains only about 20 billion pages. Hence, the deep Web is roughly 45 times larger than the surface Web. In other words, about 98% of the information on the Web is largely hidden from the view of traditional search engines. (To learn more about the deep Web, click the Deep Web Research link in the Online Companion under "Other resources.")

Finding People and Places

A variety of services on the Web allow you to search for people. At most of them, you can search for a person's phone number and street address just as you would search the white pages of a local phone book. Phone number and street address information is usually based on the information found in telephone books, which tend to be thorough and accurate. However, remember that they are not comprehensive because individuals can opt out of being listed. 🔲 You plan to attend a Department of Energy Efficiency and Renewable Energy (EERE) conference in Washington, D.C. While there, you hope to meet with a relative who you think still lives in New York City. When you explain to Bob that you want to find the relative's phone number, street address, and email address, he suggests several online directories you could try.

STEPS

QUICK TIP

You do not need to use capital letters when searching names of people, cities, businesses, and so on.

TROUBLE

If there are no results, leave the First Name text box empty or enter another name.

1. **Start your word-processing program, open the file IR D-1.doc from the drive and folder where your Data Files are located, then save it as Specialty Information in the drive and folder where you store your Data Files**
   You will use this file to record information you find in your searches.

2. **Start your browser, go to the Online Companion at www.course.com/illustrated/research4, then click the Yahoo! People Search link (under "White Pages")**
   The Yahoo! People Search home page opens, as shown in Figure D-2. You want to look for your relative, who shares your name.

3. **Under the US Phone and Address Search heading, type your first initial in the First Name/Initial text box, your last name in the Last Name text box, new york in the City/Town text box, click the State drop-down list box, scroll down and click New York, then click Phone and Address Search**
   A list of names appears, as shown in Figure D-3. Directory searches often provide better results using just an initial, rather than a first name. Notice there are sponsored results and advertisement links for advanced searches requiring you to pay a fee, which is often substantial, by using your credit card online. Your search is shown near the top of the screen, where you can make changes to the search. Near the bottom of the screen is the option to search the Web. If your results include a Map link, you can click this for directions.

4. **Choose one name and click the name in the browser window**
   A separate page opens with your person's personal data, as shown in Figure D-4.

5. **Record the chosen name and phone number in the Finding People and Places table in your document, then save the document**

6. **Click your browser's Back button twice to return to the Yahoo! People Search page**
   Although personal email addresses are not usually available, you decide to search for your relative's email address.

7. **Beneath the Email Search heading, type your first initial in the First Name/Initial text box, type your last name in the Last Name text box, then click Email Search**

8. **Use the same table to record the name you searched and whether there were any results, then save the document**

Finding personal email addresses and telephone numbers

There is no centralized service that gathers email address information. Some white pages sites search for email addresses, but, largely due to spamming, most people no longer want their email addresses available to spiders on the Web. Also, addresses tend to change frequently, even for professional or commercial sites, so addresses found through searches might be out of date. Telephone numbers can also be difficult to find for those who have opted out of being listed in telephone directories. It can be useful to try more than one directory. See the Online Companion for links to white pages directories.

FIGURE D-2: Yahoo! People Search form

First Name/Initial
text box

City/Town text box

Email Search

Reverse Phone
Number Search

Opt in and opt out options

Last Name text box

State text box

Phone and Address
Search button

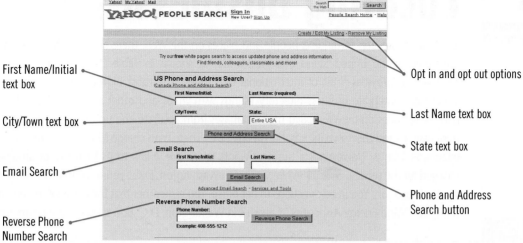

FIGURE D-3: Yahoo! People Search results (actual names and contact information blurred for privacy)

Your search

Sponsored result

Search results

Number of results

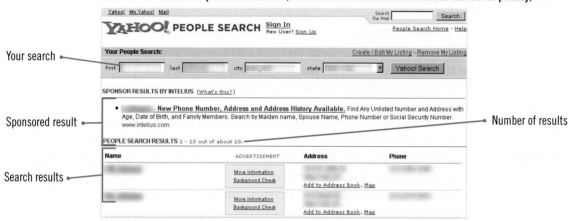

FIGURE D-4: Yahoo! Search result (actual names and contact information blurred for privacy)

Your search

Sponsored result

Search results

Finding places

Before the World Wide Web, you had to buy a map or go to the library to find out how to get where you wanted to go. Now the Web offers quite a few good map and locator Web sites. Many of these sites also provide trip planners, driving directions, and links to hotels, historical sites, and other attractions along the way. Some provide aerial views and hybrids of aerial and map views. The "Other resources" section of the Online Companion provides links to map sites with driving directions for the United States, such as Maps On Us and Yahoo! LOCAL Maps. Yahoo! and Google also cover Canada. MapQuest has sites specific to many countries, including the UK (www.mapquest.co.uk), Germany (www.mapquest.de), and France (www.mapquest.fr).

Locating Businesses

Just as there are sites for finding people and places on the Web, there are also yellow pages sites for finding businesses in the United States and worldwide, as shown in Table D-1. AnyWho (linked in the Online Companion) provides a list of international directories. The most high-powered business finders, such as SuperPages, integrate business directory listings with maps and other special features. Most of the yellow pages directories on the Web build their databases from accurate and up-to-date information and allow new businesses to add their own information at any time. There is no charge to a business for the basic address and telephone listings. However, if a business wants to include a link to its Web site or an advertisement, it is charged for the service. ▓▓▓▓▓ While you are in Washington, D.C., you hope to meet with an expert in wind energy legislation. You need directions to her office. You remember that the name of the organization is some-thing like "Wind Energy Association," and it's in Washington, D.C. Bob suggests using superpages.com.

STEPS

QUICK TIP

Find products with comparison shop-ping sites (see Shopzilla.com, PriceGrabber.com, and Shopping.com, in the Online Companion under "Other resources").

1. **Go to the Online Companion at www.course.com/illustrated/research4, then click the SuperPages link (under "Yellow Pages")**
   The SuperPages home page opens, as illustrated by Figure D-5.

2. **Click in the Or Business Name text box and type wind energy association, click in the Location text box and type washington dc, then click Find It**
   The result page is illustrated in Figure D-6. Now you'd like to see a map of the area.

3. **Click the Map link**
   Figure D-7 illustrates your result. It indicates the American Wind Energy Association building located at the center of the map. If your browser does not include this indication, use this figure to note its location.

TROUBLE

If your browser does not show the same area, you may need to zoom in or zoom out to have a similar map as shown in the figure.

4. **Note the location of the American Wind Energy Association building (on Figure D-7 if necessary) and of nearby landmarks**
   You see you are going to be about a block from The Washington Post and you decide to change your map view to get a feel for how to walk there.

5. **Click the Aerial link to change from a road map view to a real view**

6. **Note the locations of the American Wind Energy Association and The Washington Post buildings, click the plus sign (+) under Controls to zoom in twice, then use the directional control button to center the map so that both buildings are visible**

7. **Print a copy of the map, circle both buildings you plan to visit, then write your name at the top of the page**

TABLE D-1: Features of selected business finder Web sites (see the Online Companion for links)

name	country	people	business	toll-free numbers	maps	city pages
AnyWho	USA	X	X	X	X	
Canada411	Canada	X	X			
Europages	Europe		X			
Scoot	UK, France, Belgium, Netherlands		X			
SuperPages	USA	X	X		X	X
Switchboard	USA	X	X		X	X
UKphonebook	UK	X	X			
Yell.com	UK		X			
Yellowpages.ca	Canada	X	X	X		X
Yellowpages.com.au	Australia	X	X		X	

FIGURE D-5: Superpages.com home page

Yellow Pages tab is selected

Or Business Name text box

Location text box

Find It button

FIGURE D-6: Superpages.com search result

Your search

Your results

Map link

Search button

FIGURE D-7: Superpages.com map result

Plus sign (+) control button to zoom in your view

Link for Aerial view

Directional control button to move and re-center your map

Landmarks near your search result

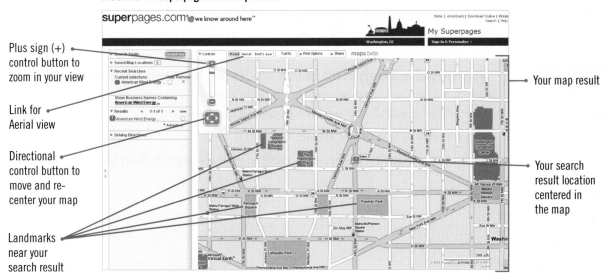

Your map result

Your search result location centered in the map

Searching Periodical Databases

Some of the most authoritative and current information hidden in the invisible Web is stored in **periodical databases**. These include the archives of magazines, newspapers, and scholarly journals. Table D-2 describes differences between types of periodicals and gives an example of each type. Some periodicals, such as *Salon* or *First Monday*, exist only in electronic format on the Web. Other periodicals, such as *The Times* or *The New York Times*, have an online version that might not carry all the same stories as the printed version and might include some stories not seen in print. Subscription databases such as ProQuest and InfoTrac, available at libraries, store electronic versions of thousands of periodical titles. Most online periodical databases provide limited recent information for free, but require payment for older materials. Some require registration. ▰▰▰▰ Before leaving for the conference in Washington, D.C., you decide to look for some current articles on alternative energy topics to read on the plane. Bob provides a list of potential databases and you decide to begin with *The Times*.

STEPS

QUICK TIP

When you use *The New York Times*, or other individual periodical indexes, you might encounter some articles that are available to subscribers only. However, your librarian can usually get these articles for you.

1. **Go to the Online Companion at www.course.com/illustrated/research4, then click The Times link (under "Periodical listings")**

   The TimesOnline home page opens.

2. **Type renewable energy in the Search text box, then click Search**

   A new TimesOnline window opens listing your search results with links to relevant articles.

3. **Scroll the results page**

   This page sorts results by relevancy, but you notice that you also have the option of sorting by date. You see that you can refine your search by entering additional keywords or clicking on listed subjects, keywords, or publication titles.

TROUBLE

If your search did not find any articles, try another search using another alternative energy topic. If your search still does not yield any articles, enter any other keywords.

4. **Click the title of an article that you think might be interesting, look at it, then record the article title in the Searching Periodical Databases table in your document**

   Next, you want to try searching a periodical database that indexes multiple titles.

5. **Go to the Online Companion, then click the MagPortal.com link (under "Periodical listings")**

   MagPortal offers broad topical categories you can navigate by drilling down to find articles of interest as well as a search engine for keyword searching of the database.

6. **In the list of subject categories, click Science & Technology, then click Environment & Geology in the list of subcategories**

   Figure D-8 shows results from drilling down through the subject categories. A Search text box is also available on your results page.

QUICK TIP

Note the annotations which help quickly identify which articles might be most useful.

7. **Type renewable energy in the Search Articles text box, then click Search**

   Figure D-9 illustrates a search results page. The small wavy line icon at the end of each article links you to similar articles. You notice that you can sort your results several ways.

8. **Click the title of one of the articles to open it**

9. **Record the article title in the same table in your document, then save your document**

FIGURE D-8: MagPortal subject categories results

Drill-down results

Option to search by keyword

Drill-down path

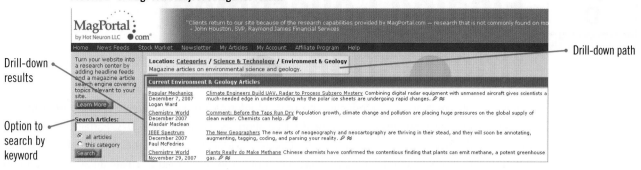

FIGURE D-9: MagPortal search results

Your search

Search results

Option to re-sort results (may be set to Quality of Match)

Click for similar articles

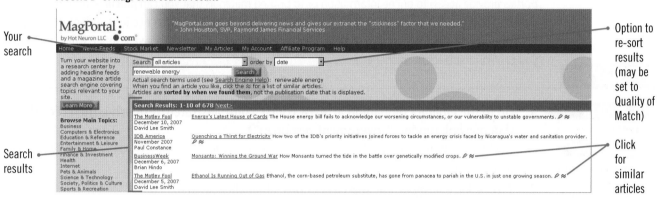

TABLE D-2: Periodicals and their distinguishing characteristics

periodical type	purpose	publisher	audience	documentation	example
Scholarly/research	Original research/ experiments	University/ organization	Scholars/ professionals/ university students	Citations/ bibliography	*Harvard Education Review*
Professional/ special interest	Professional practice/ case studies	Organization	Professionals/ university students	May cite or provide bibliography	*Journal of Accountancy*
General interest	Inform/entertain	Commercial	Knowledgeable reader/possibly technical	May mention sources	*The New York Times*
Popular	Entertain	Commercial	General audience/ simple language	Rarely mentions sources	*Metropolitan Home*

Finding online periodicals

Some sites on the Web are "online newsstands." They collect links to electronic periodicals from around the world on all topics. Examples are provided in the Online Companion under "Periodical listings." They include the Librarians' Internet Index (LII) Magazine Topics, and NewsDirectory.com. Other sites such as MagPortal.com and FindArticles allow you to search many online magazine databases simultaneously. NewsLink provides links to most U.S. newspapers as well as many magazines and international newspapers. The most comprehensive online databases, such as ProQuest and InfoTrac, are available through public, school, and academic libraries. As long as you are affiliated with a library, you can access these databases from home at no charge—just ask your local librarian for guidance.

Internet Research

Finding Government Information

Governments are prodigious producers and users of information. Large gateways, called **portals**, create access to different segments of government information, as shown in Table D-3. Portals originated in the commercial sector, with such sites as America Online and MSN that offered their version of "everything"— search engines, news, shopping, email, chat, and more. They each tried to create an attractive and useful site so that you would never go anywhere else to find information. The idea of a portal caught on and now many other sites have carved out niches in various subject areas, especially in industry and government. These portals, which are limited by subject, are also referred to as **vortals**, or vertical portals. Government portals provide access to online information or to printed materials that you can purchase from government agencies or borrow from libraries. While attending the EERE conference in Washington, D.C., you hear of a good place to access government information online—USA.gov. You want to see what information you can find there about solar energy.

STEPS

QUICK TIP

Make sure the Specialty Information document is still open in your word processor.

1. **Go to the Online Companion at www.course.com/illustrated/research4, then click the USA.gov link (under "Government resources")**
   The USA.gov Web site opens. You note that you can use either a Search text box or drill down through subject headings.

2. **Type solar energy in the Search text box, then click Search**
   A list of search results opens, as shown in Figure D-10.

3. **Scroll through the results, then record one URL in the Finding Government Information table in the Specialty Information document**

4. **Click the Advanced Search link**

5. **If your previous search is still in the search form, delete it**

6. **Type energy in the All of these words text box**

7. **Type alternative renewable green in the Any of these words text box, then click Search**
   Figure D-11 illustrates your search results.

8. **Choose one site from your results, record the URL in the same table in your document, then save the document**

Finding state and provincial government sites

You might want to use government sites for U.S. states and/or Canadian provinces. A search with "government" and the name of the state or province usually finds the official home page in the first few results.

You can also use the following portals for direct links:
- www.usa.gov/Agencies/State_and_Territories.shtml

- www.govspot.com/state/
- www.canada.gc.ca/othergov/prov_e.html

These international portals link to government pages for numerous countries:
- www.worldworld.com
- dir.yahoo.com/Government/Countries/

FIGURE D-10: USA.gov search results

Your search

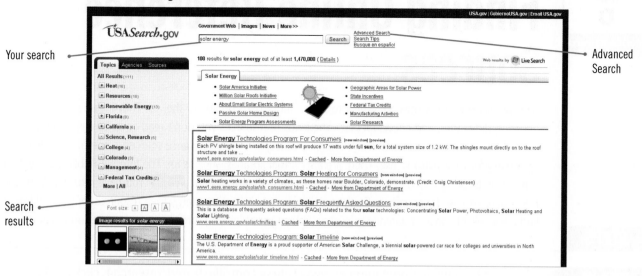

Advanced Search

Search results

FIGURE D-11: USA.gov Advanced Search results

Your search

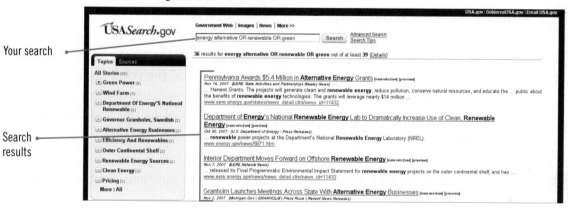

Search results

TABLE D-3: Specialized government portals (see the Online Companion)

name	features
australia.gov.au	Australian federal and state information
Government of Canada	Canadian federal, provincial, and municipal information
FedWorld (US)	Sponsored by the National Technical Information Service (NTIS) Covers scientific, technical, and engineering information Some links to government Web sites Most links to reports and publications available for purchase
USA.gov (US)	Most comprehensive site for U.S. government information Links to over 20,000 federal and state government Web sites
DirectGov	Central and local government information for the United Kingdom
GPO Access	Links to federal publications Provides catalog of government documents available for purchase Catalog of libraries that own specific documents
University of Michigan Documents Center	Most complete guide to government information
	Links to local, state, national, and international government sites

Finding Online Reference Sources

Online reference sources are similar to their counterparts on library shelves. They include almanacs, dictionaries, directories, and encyclopedias—the kinds of resources you don't read cover to cover, but refer to often. Library Web sites almost always link to a variety of online reference sources, some of them licensed exclusively for their patrons' use. There are also virtual libraries, such as ipl, The Internet Public Library, that exist solely to bring together valuable Web sites and reference tools. ▰▰▰▰ You have returned from the EERE conference and are ready to finish your final list of alternative energy Web resources, but would like to find a few reliable online reference resources. Bob suggests looking through the reference sources at ipl.

STEPS

QUICK TIP

It's a good idea, when you find good reference sites, to add them to your browser's Favorites or Bookmarks file for easy access.

1. **Go to the Online Companion at www.course.com/illustrated/research4, click the ipl Reference Page link (under "Online references"), then click Subject Collections**
   The Internet Public Library main subject categories page appears. You see that ipl offers both a search engine and subject headings to drill through.

2. **Click in the Search text box, type energy, then click Search**
   Figure D-12 illustrates your results.

3. **Examine how your results are sorted, click Advanced Search under the Search text box, click the Grok It tab, type energy in the Search for text box, then click Search**
   Your results are now sorted into an outline view or a map view which clusters results into subject subcategories.

4. **In Outline View, click Solar Energy, choose a site, then record the URL in the Finding Online Reference Sources table in the Specialty Information document**
   Now you decide to drill down through ipl's subjects to compare your results.

TROUBLE

Web sites are redesigned frequently. Click a similar link if this exact one is not there.

5. **Click your browser's Back button to return to ipl's home page, then click the Science link under Subject Collections**

6. **Click Energy in the Science subheadings, browse the resources, choose one link that seems helpful for your project, then record the URL in the Finding Online Reference Sources table in your document**
   Figure D-13 illustrates the ipl Energy resources page. You want to see more links to online reference resources.

7. **Click your browser's Back button to return to the Online Companion, then click the Librarians' Internet Index link (under "Subject guides")**

8. **Click Science in the list of subject headings on the LII homepage**

9. **Click Environment in the list of Science subheadings, then click Energy in the list of subheadings under Science: Environment**

10. **Choose one URL, record it in the same table in your document, then save the document**

FIGURE D-12: ipl search results

Search text box

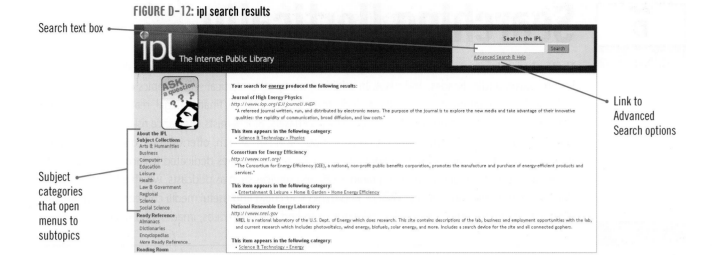

Link to
Advanced
Search options

Subject
categories
that open
menus to
subtopics

FIGURE D-13: ipl subject drill down

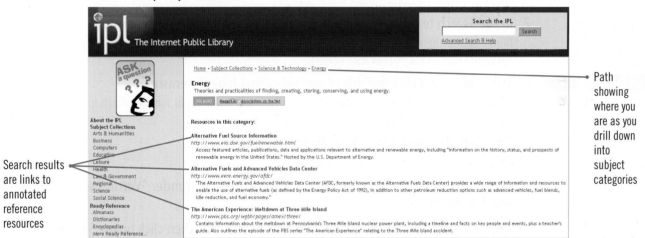

Search results
are links to
annotated
reference
resources

Path
showing
where you
are as you
drill down
into
subject
categories

Finding online reference sources about the Internet

The Web includes reference sources on just about any topic. If you are working on a special research topic, you can always find good sources at the Reference sections of The Internet Public Library or the Librarians' Internet Index and add them temporarily to your browser's Bookmark or Favorite files. For instance, if you were studying the Internet, the following might be good sources to have close at hand:

name	resource type	features
FILExt	Dictionary	Lists most Internet file extensions; defines extensions and links to more information
Netiquette Home Page	Book	Provides the basics of Netiquette, at work and at home; covers primarily online communication
Webopedia	Dictionary/ encyclopedia	Covers computer and Internet terminology; provides paragraph definitions and links
Living Internet	Encyclopedia	Covers the Internet, the Web, email, chat, newsgroups, and mailing lists; articles include history and how-to information
Internet Tutorials (Univ. of Albany Libraries)	Tutorial	Covers using the Web, searching the Web, browsers, and training; provides links and how-to tips
LII.org (Internet Guides and Search Tools Page)	Subject guide	Provides reliable links to answer almost any Internet question; covers searching, Web design, history, law, children, and more

Searching Vertically

Vertical search focuses on a specific category of media or content. Some popular vertical search categories include video, audio, images, and news. In addition, many other vertical search topics exist, such as shopping, health, local information, job listings, industry (e.g., automotive, finance, legal, real estate, and travel), academic, maps, and professional (e.g., corporate purchasers, biochemists, insurance risk assessors, and psychiatrists). The largest search engines, Google, Yahoo!, and Live Search, offer options to perform the more popular types of vertical searches. In addition, specialty search engines dedicated to locating specific categories of media or content are growing rapidly, offering services such as podcasts, which provide automatic downloads of media and content. Bob thinks you could find useful media content about alternative energy. He suggests you use vertical search engines to find relevant videos, images, and news items.

STEPS

1. **Go to the Online Companion at www.course.com/illustrated/research4, then click blinkx (under "Vertical search engines:" and "Video")**
   Figure D-14 illustrates the blinkx home page.

2. **In the Search text box, type "alternative energy sources", then click Go**
   Blinkx shows the number of videos found, shows thumbnail videos next to each result, and provides options to sort results by relevance or date.

QUICK TIP
You might need to turn on your computer speakers to hear the video.

3. **Scroll down and click the title of any video that looks interesting**
   A browser window will open and begin playing the video. You might have to watch a commercial before your selected video begins.

4. **After watching the video, close the browser window**
   The blinkx search results window reappears.

5. **Go to the Online Companion, then click Yahoo! Images (under "Vertical search engines:" and "Images")**

6. **Click in the Search text box, type "alternative energy", then click Image Search**
   Your search results appear, displaying thumbnail pictures and image sizes, as illustrated in Figure D-15.

7. **Go to the Online Companion, click Google News (under "Vertical search engines:" and "News"), click in the Search text box, type "alternative energy", then click Search News**
   Your search results appear, displaying news item titles, dates, and descriptions, as shown in Figure D-16. Results can be sorted by date or relevance and can be limited to items from the last hour, the last day, the past week, the past month, or the past year.

8. **Scroll down and click an appropriate item**

9. **Print a copy of the first page, then write your name at the top of the page**

Understanding blended search

Blended or universal search combines traditional Web and vertical search results (e.g., video, audio, images, news, maps, and so on) into one comprehensive result page. This makes it easer and faster to locate information about a topic from a wide variety of media.

However, blended search results can introduce irrelevant results that might not be of interest. The major search engines, including Google, Yahoo!, and Microsoft Live Search, all use blended search and there is currently no way to switch it off.

FIGURE D-14: Blinkx home page

FIGURE D-15: Yahoo! Image search results

Options to search other kinds of content

Your search

Search results are thumbnail images

Option for Advanced Search

Number of results

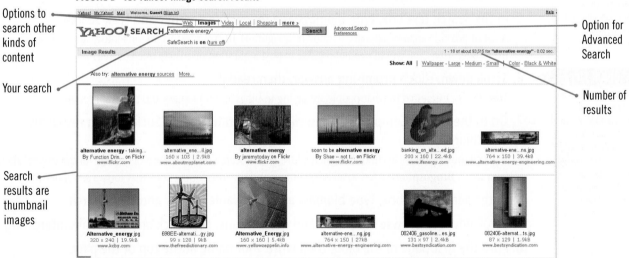

FIGURE D-16: Google News search results

Your search

Ways to limit search results

Search results

Option for Advanced Search

Number of results

Options to re-sort results

Options for displaying your results

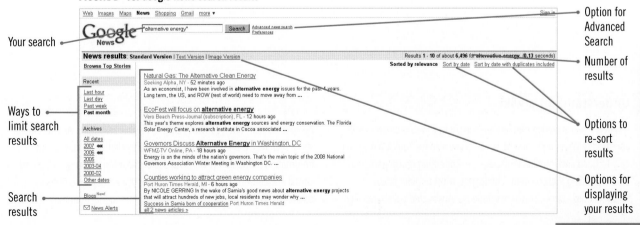

Internet Research

Joining the Social Search

Social search relies on community participation and human judgment to locate information of common interest and answer specific questions. Social search works well for finding subjective material that requires informed opinions. Common forms of social search include **blogs**, **social bookmarking** (or **tagging**) sites, **collaborative harvesters**, and **question-and-answer (Q&A)** sites. See Table D-4 for descriptions and examples of common forms of social search. At the EERE conference, you met experts in biomass as a renewable energy. Bob suggests social searching to find other informed opinions on this subject.

STEPS

QUICK TIP

Be discriminating when sharing personal information on social sites, or you might open yourself to spam, phishing, or other attacks.

1. **Go to the Online Companion at www.course.com/illustrated/research4, then click Del.icio.us (under "Social search resources:" and "Bookmarking sites")**

2. **In the Search text box, type biomass renewable energy and click Search**

   A list of people's bookmarks appears, containing tags (single-word descriptors) that match your keywords, as illustrated in Figure D-17. Tags for each bookmark are displayed, along with the total number of people who have saved the link, indicating its popularity.

3. **Scroll down, click a useful link that has been saved by a significant number of people, then briefly explore the information**

   You now want to see answers to questions about biomass as a renewable energy.

QUICK TIP

Another means of posting questions and receiving answers is in online discussion groups, such as Google Groups and Yahoo! Groups.

4. **Go to the Online Companion, then click Yahoo! Answers (under "Social search resources:" and "Q&A sites")**

5. **In the Search text box, type biomass as a renewable energy? and click Search**

   A list of possible answers appears, as shown in Figure D-18. Your results are previously answered questions from other users. You would need to register to post a question or answer one yourself.

QUICK TIP

Some blogs are general or personal. Some are specific to topic and audience. Although most go unread, some are must-reads within specific professional or cultural groups.

6. **Scroll down, click a promising answer, then read it**

   You are also interested in what people are saying in blogs about biomass and renewable energy.

7. **Go to the Online Companion, then click Technorati (under "Social search resources:" and "Blogs")**

   A search form opens for Technorati, which allows you to search much of the blogosphere for discussions about your topic. **Blogosphere** refers to all blog content and the interconnections that form a social network.

8. **In the Search text box, type biomass as a renewable energy and click Search**

9. **Scroll down to browse blog titles and descriptions, then click one that looks interesting**

10. **Print the first page of the blog, then write your name at the top of the page**

Understanding a wiki

A wiki is server software that lets anyone using a Web browser create and modify Web page content. A wiki (Hawaiian for "quick") makes it easy to build and interlink Web pages, encouraging group participation in building Web content. The largest, most popular one is Wikipedia.org, a free online encyclopedia constructed collaboratively by volunteers. It often provides links to reliable resources. As with other social searches, it is important to check authoritative sources about information found in a wiki if your use of the information goes beyond casual interest. Any group communication tool that allows users to create and edit content risks accidental or intentional misinformation.

FIGURE D-17: Del.icio.us search results

Your search

Related tags

Search results

Sponsored results

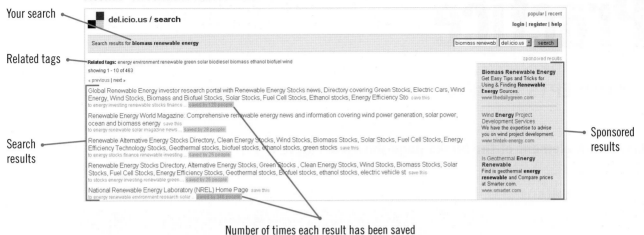

Number of times each result has been saved

FIGURE D-18: Yahoo! Answers search results

Your search

Registration required to ask new questions or submit answers

Search results are previously asked and answered questions

Sponsored results

TABLE D-4: Social search resources (see the Online Companion for links to these social sites)

social search types	description	examples
Blogs	Sites where people post commentaries and invite comments; blog search engines quickly find posts about almost any topic	Blogdigger Bloglines Blog Street Google Blog Search Technorati
(Social) Bookmarking sites	Sites where people store and describe their favorite Web pages with descriptors (tags), allowing you to search for popular content	Del.icio.us Diigo Gravee Simpy Spurl.net
Collaborative harvesters	Tools that aggregate forms of social search, letting users nominate and vote on content; search results are ranked by popularity	Digg Popurls Propeller Reddit Tailrank
Q&A (question-and-answer) sites	Sites where people pose a question and receive answers back from anyone willing and (hopefully) knowledgeable enough to reply	Answers.com Answerbag.com Help.com Live QnA WikiAnswers Wondir Yahoo! Answers

Practice

▼ CONCEPTS REVIEW

Label each element of the blinkx page shown in Figure D-19.

FIGURE D-19

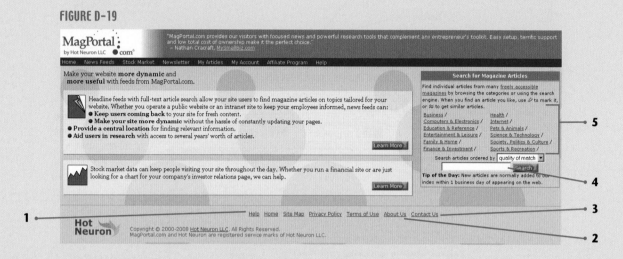

Match each term with the statement that best describes it.

6. **Visible Web**
7. **Dynamic Web page**
8. **White pages**
9. **Yellow pages**
10. **The Internet Public Library**
11. **Portal**
12. **Social search**
13. **Vertical search**
14. **Invisible Web**

a. Web sites with "people finder" tools
b. An example of a virtual library
c. A gateway to large segments of related Web information
d. Allows you to focus on finding specific media types, such as video, audio, images, news
e. The portion of the Web not accessible to traditional search engines
f. Uses community participation and human judgment to locate information of common interest and answer specific questions
g. The portion of the Web accessible to traditional search engines and directories
h. Web sites that help you find businesses
i. A Web page that is generated when you request it

Select the best answer from the list of choices.

15. The invisible Web:
  a. Is not accessible.
  b. Consists mostly of dynamically generated Web pages.
  c. Is much smaller than the visible Web.
  d. Is also known as the deep Web.

16. You would not usually access specialty research tools by:
  a. Asking a librarian.
  b. Using a search engine.
  c. Using a library's Web site.
  d. Using a virtual library site.

17. Specialty sites might:
  a. Require you to pay for the service.
  b. Allow you a few free searches and ask you to pay for more.
  c. Give away some information but charge for some too.
  d. All of the above

18. Up-to-date, detailed information about people and businesses is often:
  a. Hard to come by.
  b. Valuable.
  c. Protected by companies with security measures because of its proprietary nature.
  d. All of the above

19. You would usually look for _____ at an online White Pages site.
  a. A person's address
  b. A person's email address
  c. A person's phone number
  d. All of the above

20. A good place to search for information about businesses in the UK and France is:
  a. The Librarians' Internet Index.
  b. Scoot.
  c. Yellowpages.ca.
  d. Switchboard.

21. Common forms of social search include:
  a. Question-and-answer sites.
  b. Blogs.
  c. Monitoring and polling people's opinions.
  d. All of the above

22. A site that links to local, state, national, and international government links is:
  a. FirstGov.
  b. University of Michigan Documents Center.
  c. FedWorld.
  d. United States Government Printing Office.

23. Blinkx is an example of:
  a. A government Web site.
  b. A subject guide.
  c. A video search engine.
  d. A Yellow Pages site.

24. Del.icio.us is an example of:
  a. A Yellow Pages site.
  b. A White Pages site.
  c. An audio search engine.
  d. A social bookmarking (tagging) site.

▼ SKILLS REVIEW

1. **Understand specialty information.**
  a. Start your word-processing program, open the file IR D-2.doc from the drive and folder where your Data Files are located, then save it as **Specialty Searches**.
  b. Use the Skill #1 table in your document to write a brief description of the invisible or Deep Web.
  c. In the same table, list three sources that search the deep Web.

2. **Find people and places.**
  a. Go to the Online Companion at www.course.com/illustrated/research4, then click the 411 Locate link under "White Pages."
  b. In the White Pages Search form, type your first and last name (or a friend's name) into the appropriate text boxes.
  c. Click Search.

    d. Click your name (or your friend's name) on the results page. If there are no results, try a different name.

    e. Print the resulting page of information, then write your name at the top of the page.

3. Locate businesses.

    a. In the Online Companion, click the Switchboard link under "Yellow Pages," then, if necessary, click Find a Business.

    b. Type a business category (such as accountants, newspapers, schools, or veterinarians), a city, and a state, then click Search. (If there are no resulting businesses, go back and enter another type of business.)

    c. Scroll down the results page and choose a business.

    d. Click the Map link for that business.

    e. Print the map, then write your name at the top of the page. (You might need to click a link saying something like Print View, or Printable Map, to get a good copy.)

4. Search periodical databases.

    a. In the Online Companion, click the MagPortal.com link under "Periodical listings."

    b. Search for a magazine article by typing your search terms in the Search text box.

    c. Scan the list of resulting articles and record one URL in the Skill #4 table in your document.

    d. In the Online Companion, click the New York Times link under "Periodical listings."

    e. Search for another article on the same topic.

    f. Scan the list of resulting articles and record one URL in the Skill #4 table in your document.

    g. Save and close the document, then exit your word-processing program.

5. Find government information.

    a. In the Online Companion, click the USA.gov link under "Government resources."

    b. Click Search to get to the main search form screen.

    c. Click Advanced Search.

    d. Type **senator** in the All of these words text box.

    e. Click the Search in list box, scroll down, then click Washington.

    f. Click Search.

    g. Find a Web page with a state senator's name on it, print the page, then write your name at the top of the page.

6. Find online reference sources.

    a. In the Online Companion, click the ipl Reference Page under "Online references."

    b. Click More Ready Reference (under Ready Reference), then click the Style & Writing Guides link.

    c. Click the link to APA.

    d. Find a Web site that can help you cite documents in the APA style.

    e. Click the page name, print a copy of the first page, then write your name at the top of the page.

7. Search vertically.

    a. In the Online Companion, click the blinkx link under "Vertical search engines" and "Video."

    b. In the Search text box, type "**Internet search**" then click Go.

    c. Scroll down the results page and click a video that interests you.

    d. After you watch the video, go to the Online Companion, click the Google News link under "Vertical search engines" and "News."

    e. In the Search text box, type "**Internet search**" then click Search News.

    f. Scroll down and click a news item of interest.

    g. Read the news article, print a copy of the first page, then write your name at the top of the page.

8. Join the social search.

    a. In the Online Companion, click the WikiAnswers link under "Social search resources" and "Q&A sites."

    b. In the Search text box, type **What is a blog?**, then click Go.

    c. Read the answer.

    d. Go to the Online Companion, then click the Google Blog Search link under "Social search resources" and "Blogs."

    e. In the Search text box, type **Social Search**, then click Search Blogs.

f. Explore several of the blogs.

g. Print the first page of your search results, as shown in Figure D-20, then write your name at the top of the page.

▼ INDEPENDENT CHALLENGE 1

You and a business associate are driving from London to York to visit some clients. As you haven't driven there before, you want to get driving directions.

a. Go to the Online Companion at www.course.com/illustrated/research4, then click the MapQuest UK link (under "Other resources").

b. Find the section for driving directions.

c. Enter the appropriate to and from locations and get the directions.

d. On the resulting directions page, as shown in Figure D-21, locate the Printer Friendly link, then click the link.

e. Print a copy of the directions, then write your name at the top of the page.

Advanced Challenge Exercise

- While looking for maps, you decide to check the driving distance across Canada.

- Return to the Online Companion, click the MapQuest USA link, then click the Driving Directions icon. Note the driving distance between Quebec, QC, and Vancouver, BC.

- You realize the mileage quoted is while traveling much of the way in the United States. Because you particularly want the drive to remain in Canada, restate your query in several shorter trips to keep the directions within Canada. (*Hint*: If you want, you can use Quebec, QC, to Sudbury, ON, then Sudbury to Winnipeg, MB, then Winnipeg to Vancouver, BC.)

- Print a copy of your final driving directions, then write the total trip mileage and your name at the top of the page.

FIGURE D-20

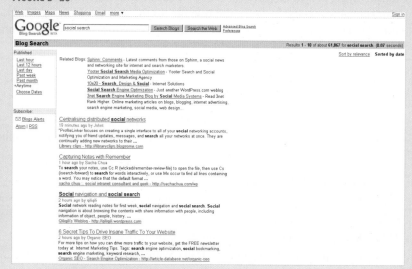

FIGURE D-21

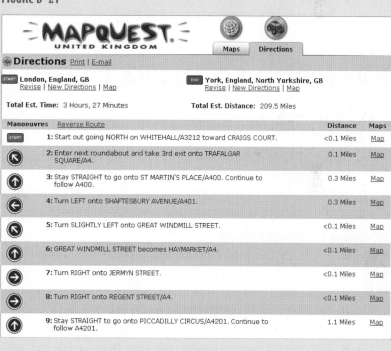

▼ INDEPENDENT CHALLENGE 2

You are flying to Sydney, NSW, Australia, on business. You are with a firm that specializes in designing Web sites for banks. Your company is going to design the Web site for the Waratah Mortgage Corporation, and you decide to check the Web for other banks you might visit while in the Sydney Metro area. You look up phone numbers and locations of banks on your laptop.

a. Go to the Online Companion at www.course.com/illustrated/research4, then click the Yellowpages.com.au link under "Yellow pages."

b. From the information you know, set up an appropriate search.

c. Print the search results, which shows a list of banks, their phone numbers, and a map of the area, then write your name at the top of the page.

Advanced Challenge Exercise

■ You want to check out the competition in the area.

■ Use the Yellowpages.com.au site to find companies located in the Greater Sydney NSW that design Web sites, as shown in Figure D-22.

■ Explore the descriptions for several of the Web site design businesses.

■ Return to the search results, print the first page of results, then write your name at the top of the page.

FIGURE D-22

▼ INDEPENDENT CHALLENGE 3

You are thinking of immigrating to Canada and starting a business. You have heard there is a special business class immigration available.

a. Go to the Online Companion at www.course.com/illustrated/research4, then click the Government of Canada link under "Government references."

b. Locate an official Canadian government Web page that has the information you need.

c. Print the page, then write your name at the top of the page.

Advanced Challenge Exercise

■ You decide to compare the immigration and business opportunities in Australia with those in Canada.

■ Go to the Online Companion, then click the australia.gov.au link under "Government references."

■ In the Search text box, type **immigration business class**, then click Go.

■ Explore the results until you find a page that contains information about immigrating to Australia to start a business, print it, then write your name at the top of the page.

■ Compare the business immigration pages from Canada and Australia. You conclude that both countries are interested in attracting people to come and start new businesses.

▼ REAL LIFE INDEPENDENT CHALLENGE

Job interviews have become highly competitive, with tougher questions, better trained interviewers, and well-prepared applicants. Your chances of performing well in a job interview can be improved with practice and insightful tips. You decide to use a vertical search engine to find visual demonstrations and advice on how to practice for a job interview.

- **a.** Go to the Online Companion, then click the blinkx link under "Vertical search engines" and "Video."
- **b.** In the Search text box, type **how practice "job interview"** as shown in Figure D-23, then click Go.
- **c.** Scroll down the list of videos on the results page and find one with a title that looks useful.
- **d.** Watch the video, then go back to the search results and check out another promising video.
- **e.** Return to the first search results page, print it, then write your name at the top of the page.

FIGURE D-23

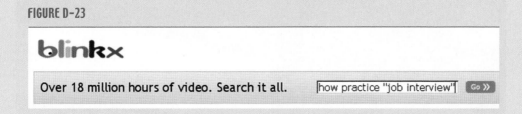

▼ VISUAL WORKSHOP

Now that you know how to search the invisible Web, use a vertical search engine to find a famous photograph of your favorite hockey player after he scored the winning goal in the 1970 Stanley Cup final. You know this goal, scored by Bobby Orr, is referred to as "the goal" and you know the picture you want was taken by a photographer from the Boston Globe newspaper. Perform an image search in Google to locate the page illustrated in Figure D-24 (*Hints*: The link to the vertical search engine site is listed in the Online Companion. The most efficient search query will consist of three phrases). When you find this page, print it, then write your name at the top of the page.

FIGURE D-24

Galleries >> Sports >> Bobby Orr The Goal

Frank O'Brien/Globe Staff

1970 Stanley Cup Finals — Boston vs. St. Louis — Boston Garden — Bobby Orr scores winning goal to win Stanley Cup.

Glossary

Algorithm A mathematical formula used by a search engine to rank each Web site returned in search results according to the terms used in the search query.

AND A Boolean operator that connects keywords in a search query. AND narrows a search and decreases the number of search results because each keyword connected with AND must be on a Web page for it to be included in the results. Every additional keyword connected to a search by AND further narrows the search. *Note:* Most search tools use AND as the default Boolean operator, so entering it in your search query usually is unnecessary. If you're unsure how a search tool uses AND or the plus sign (+), read the tool's Help pages. *See also* Boolean operators.

AND NOT A Boolean operator that connects keywords in a search query. Using AND NOT narrows a search and decreases the number of search results because each word must not be on a Web page for it to be included in the results. Every additional keyword connected to a search by AND NOT further narrows the search. *Note:* Most search tools require the use of the minus sign (–) to indicate AND NOT. If you're unsure how a search tool uses AND NOT or the minus sign (–), read the tool's Help pages. *See also* Boolean operators.

Annotation A summary or review of a Web page, usually written by experts, such as professionals, academics in the field, or librarians.

Blended search Web and vertical search results (e.g., video, audio, images, news, maps, and so on) are combined into one comprehensive result page.

Blogosphere All blog content and the interconnections that form a social network.

Blogs Web sites where people post commentaries and others respond by posting their opinions in reaction to the commentary.

Bookmarks A browser function, in Firefox, Opera, and Safari, that allows for easy storage, organization, and revisiting of Web pages. This browser feature is called Favorites in Internet Explorer.

Boolean logic A logic system, based on simple algebra and developed by mathematician George Boole, which defines how Boolean operators manipulate sets of data. It is also known as Boolean algebra and is represented graphically with Venn diagrams.

Boolean operators Command words such as AND, OR, and AND NOT that narrow, expand, or restrict a search based on Boolean logic.

Cached page A copy of a Web page that resides on a search engine's computer.

Citation format A style guide that standardizes references to resources like books, magazine articles, and Web pages. Common formats are those by MLA (Modern Language Association) and APA (American Psychological Association).

Collaborative harvesters Tools that aggregate forms of social search, letting users nominate and vote on content. Search results are ranked by popularity.

Complex query A search query that uses Boolean operators to define the relationships between keywords and phrases in a way that search tools can interpret.

Corporate author A committee, association, or group credited with creating a work such as a Web page.

Deep Web *See* Invisible Web.

Default operator The Boolean operator that a search engine automatically uses in a query, whether typed as part of the query or not. Most search engines default to the AND operator, although a few default to the OR operator.

Dewey Decimal system A numeric subject classification system used in many libraries. Named after its inventor Melville Dewey.

Directory *See* Subject guide.

Discussion board A virtual bulletin board that organizes messages by topic and allows users to post and respond to messages.

Distributed subject guide A subject guide created by a variety of editors working somewhat independently and usually stored on numerous computers around the country or the world. Like a regular subject guide, it hierarchically arranges links to Web pages based on topics and subtopics. Though many distributed subject guides are excellent, they often lack standardization and can be uneven in quality. *See also* Subject guide.

Domain The last two or three letters of a URL. URLs from the United States typically end in three letters, indicating the type of site, such as *.gov*, *.edu*, *.org*, or *.com*. URLs from other countries typically end in two letters, indicating the country of origin, such as *.ca* (*Canada*), *.uk* (*United Kingdom*), or *.jp* (*Japan*).

Drilling down Clicking through subject headings (or topics or categories) to reach relevant links. Typically the subject topics are arranged from the more general to the more specific.

Dynamically generated Web pages Pages generated by a database in response to a specific query. One kind of page found in the invisible Web.

Evaluative criteria Standards used to determine if a Web site is appropriate for your needs. These standards usually include considerations of organization, authority, objectivity, accuracy, scope, and currency.

Favorites A function of the Internet Explorer browser that allows for easy storage, organization, and revisiting of Web pages. This feature is called Bookmarks in Firefox, Opera, and Safari.

Filter *See* Search filter.

Forcing the order of operation Using parentheses in a complex query to force the search tool to look at the words inside the parentheses first, which can greatly affect search results. If not forced, search tools typically search keywords from left to right.

Hierarchy A ranked order. Hierarchies commonly used in Internet subject guides include topical, alphabetical, and geographical. Topical hierarchies typically go from the more general to the more specific.

HTML (Hypertext Markup Language) A coded format language used to create and control the appearance of documents on the Web. *See also* Web page.

Internet A vast global network of interconnected networks that allows you to find and connect to information on the Web.

Internet directory *See* Subject guide.

Internet search tools Services that help locate information on the Web, including search engines, metasearch engines, subject guides, and specialized search tools.

Intersection The place where two sets overlap in a Venn diagram. Results from the use of the Boolean AND.

Invisible Web The part of the Web inaccessible to search engine spiders. It consists primarily of information housed in databases. Also called the Deep web.

Keyword An important word that describes a major concept of your search topic.

Listserv A software program that supports interactive Internet communication, such as the use of mailing lists.

Metasearch engine A search tool that searches the indexes of multiple search engines simultaneously. Better metasearch engines, such as ixquick and ProFusion, present your query to various search engines in the ways they will understand it. Because most do not, it is usually best to metasearch with only simple searches.

Minus sign Used by many search tools as a symbol for the Boolean AND NOT.

Mnemonic Assisting or aiding memory. For example, many URLs are mnemonic to make them easier to remember.

Online reference sources Digital versions of almanacs, dictionaries, encyclopedias, and other similar resources available on the Internet.

OR A Boolean operator that connects keywords in a search query. Using OR broadens or expands a search and increases the number of search results because any of the words can be on a Web page for it to be included in the results. Every additional keyword connected to a search by OR further broadens the search. *See also* Boolean operators.

Order of operation *See* Forcing the order of operation.

Parentheses Used around two or more keywords combined with Boolean operators, parentheses force the order of operation of a search query by indicating that the part of the search inside the parentheses should be performed first.

Periodical database A specialized database that contains the full text of articles from periodicals, such as newspapers, magazines, and journals. Common periodical databases are ProQuest, InfoTrac, and EbscoHost. This kind of database usually requires a paid subscription and is only available at libraries.

Phrase searching Forcing the search tool to search only for pages containing a phrase, or two or more words together in a certain order. Typically quotation marks are used around the words to indicate that they should be searched as a phrase. Phrases can be used with Boolean operators in the same ways a keyword can be used.

Plus sign Used by many search tools to indicate the Boolean AND. Because AND is the default operator for most search tools, it is usually unnecessary to enter it in your search query. *See also* AND.

Podcasts A software system that lets users subscribe to automatic downloads of media content.

Portal A large Web gateway providing access to huge amounts of information. It often includes search engines, news, shopping, email, chat, and more. A portal that focuses on one topic or industry is called a vertical portal or a vortal.

Query *See* Search query.

Question-and-answer site A social search tool that lets you pose a question and receive answers back from anyone willing and (hopefully) knowledgeable enough to reply.

Quotation marks Used around two or more keywords in a search form, quotation marks indicate to most search tools that the words should be searched as a phrase.

Scope The range of topics covered by a Web site. The scope of a site might be narrow, covering a smaller range of topics, or broad, covering a wider range of topics.

Search engine A search tool, usually indexed by spiders, that locates Web pages containing the keywords entered in a search form.

Search filter A program used by search tools, usually from Advanced Search pages, to specifically include or exclude Web pages according to criteria such as language, file format, date, and domain. Whenever a filter is used, results are limited. Every additional filter used in a search further limits the results.

Search form The place where a user enters a search query at a search tool. It can be one text box or a complex array of text boxes, filters, and drop-down menus.

Search query Keywords, phrases, and/or Boolean operators entered into a search form that the search tool uses to search its index.

Search results The Web pages the search tool returns in response to a search.

Semantic Web A universal platform that encodes meaning (semantics) into the content of the Web.

Set The term used for a group in Boolean logic. In a Venn diagram, a set is commonly represented as a circle.

Social bookmarking Sites where people store and describe their favorite Web pages with descriptors (tags), allowing you to search for popular content. Also called tagging.

Social search Finding answers to specific questions and locating information of common interest using human judgment and community participation.

Specialized search engine A search engine that limits the Web pages it indexes by subject. A specialized search engine often combines the power of Boolean searching with the focus of a subject guide.

Specialized search tool A Web site that provides access to data stored in online databases that require direct access, making traditional search engines and most subject guides ineffective. Specialized search tools include those that search online telephone directories, reference tools, online maps, and online periodicals.

Spider A computer program that scans, or crawls, the Web to index Web pages. The spider-created index is searched when you query a search engine. Spiders do not make judgments regarding the value of indexing a page as human indexers do.

Stop words Common words, such as *a, and, the, for,* and *of,* that are not normally searched by search tools.

Subject directory *See* Subject guide.

Subject guide A search tool that hierarchically arranges links to Web pages. The links are evaluated and annotated by people, usually subject specialists or librarians, as opposed to spiders. Also called subject directory, subject index, or subject tree.

Subject index *See* Subject guide.

Subject tree *See* Subject guide.

Subscription A payment made to the owner or distributor of digital information for online access for a specified period of time, usually a year.

Surface Web *See* Visible Web.

Synonyms Words that have similar meanings. In an online search, synonyms are normally used to expand a search. They are usually connected by the Boolean operator OR.

Syntax Rules of a language, like grammar, that standardize usage. In computer searching, syntax governs the form queries must take to instruct a search tool to perform a certain function.

Tagging *See* Social bookmarking.

Thread A subtopic of newsgroup postings. A discussion starts with one posting. Subsequent postings in response to it, no matter how many there are, are considered one thread.

Trailblazer page A Web page that links to numerous sites covering all aspects of a topic. Often trailblazer pages are compiled by experts in a field.

Union The combination of two sets in a Venn diagram. Results from use of the Boolean OR.

Venn diagrams Drawings, typically comprised of interacting circles, used to illustrate Boolean logic or searches using Boolean operators. First developed by mathematician John Venn.

Vertical search Finding video, audio, images, and news by focusing on specific media.

Visible Web The portion of the Web that is indexed by search engine spiders. Also might refer to parts of the Web that, although not crawled by spiders, are indexed by subject guides. The visible Web, also known as the surface Web, is hundreds of times smaller than the invisible or deep Web.

Vortal A vertical portal. *See also* Portal.

Web *See* World Wide Web.

Web page The most common type of document on the World Wide Web. Most results from search engines and subject guides are Web pages, which are usually written in Hypertext Markup Language, or HTML, and have file extensions of .htm or .html. Other types of file formats include .pdf (Adobe Acrobat), .ppt, .pptx (PowerPoint), .xls, .xlsx (Excel), .doc and .docx (Word).

Web site Stores, links, and delivers Web pages. A Web site can range in size from one Web page to thousands of Web pages.

World Wide Web An enormous repository of information stored on millions of computers all over the world.

Index